Virginia Woolf
Life and London
A Biography of Place

Virginia Woolf
Life and London
A Biography of Place by
Jean Moorcroft Wilson
Illustrated by Leonard McDermid

W · W · NORTON & COMPANY
New York   London

Printed in the United States of America.

Library of Congress Cataloging-in-Publication Data

Wilson, Jean Moorcraft.
Virginia Woolf, life and London: a biography of place / by Jean
Moorcraft Wilson: illustrated by Leonard McDermid.
p. cm.
Bibliography: p.
Includes index.
1. Woolf, Virginia, 1882–1941—Homes and haunts—England—London.
2. Literary landmarks—England—London. 3. London (England) in
literature. 4. London (England)—Description. 5. Novelists,
English—20th century—Biography. I. Title.
PR6045.072Z92 1988
823'.912—dc19
[B]   88-19601

ISBN 0-393-02615-9

W. W. Norton & Company, Inc., 500 Fifth Avenue, New York, N.Y. 10110
W. W. Norton & Company Ltd., 37 Great Russell Street, London WC1B 3NU

1 2 3 4 5 6 7 8 9 0

For
Cecil,
Kate, Philip, Emma,
Alice and Trim
Woolf

Acknowledgements

My greatest debts are to my husband, who encouraged me to write this book, and to Professor Harold Brooks, in particular for his advice with the second section.

A number of people were of invaluable assistance when it came to 'recreating' those of Virginia Woolf's houses now demolished. First and foremost I must thank Leonard McDermid for spending so many hours studying old photographs and reproducing them so vividly. I should also like to thank David Richards of the Local History department of Holborn Library, who supplied me both with photographs and information, the Local History department of both Swiss Cottage and Richmond Central Reference Libraries and Christopher Denvir of the Greater London Record Office and History Library. The present owners of the Round House, Lewes, were extremely welcoming and informative when I called on them unexpectedly; and Hugh Lee, the Editor of *The Charleston Newsletter*, could not have been more encouraging and helpful. I am also very grateful to Vicki Walton, the Curator of Charleston, for her co-operation, which went far beyond the bounds of duty.

For permission to quote from Virginia Woolf's *Diaries* and *Letters*, *The Voyage Out*, *Night and Day*, *Jacob's Room*, *Mrs Dalloway*, *Orlando*, *The Waves*, *The Years*, *Moments of Being*, *The London Scene* and Leonard Woolf's *Sowing* and *Beginning Again* I here make acknowledgement to Chatto & Windus, The Hogarth Press, copyright The Estate of Virginia Woolf.

J.M.W.

Contents

Illustrations

Introduction

London is enchanting. I step out upon a tawny coloured magic carpet, it seems, and get carried into beauty
without raising a finger. The nights are amazing, with
all the white porticos and broad silent avenues. And
people pop in and out, lightly, divertingly like rabbits;
and I look down Southampton Row, wet as a seal's
back or red and yellow with sunshine, and watch the
omnibuses going and coming and hear the old crazy
organs. One of these days I will write about London,
and how it takes up the private life and carries it on,
without any effort. Faces passing lift up my mind;
prevent it from settling, as it does in the stillness of
Rodmell.

Virginia Woolf never followed up her idea of a book
about London, though she did write a number of essays
on what was for her more than a city, more even than a
home. London is for Virginia quite simply 'the centre of
things'. By this she means not merely a commercial or
social centre but the centre of life itself. London has for
her a mystical significance; it is a symbol of what she
variously calls 'life', 'truth' or 'reality', a quality she is
trying to identify in her life and to capture in her work.
Irritated as she is at times by London's noise, dirt and
frenzy, Virginia ultimately sees it as vital, in every sense
of that word. One of her characters, Mrs Dalloway,
vividly expresses Virginia's own deep feelings about
London:

Such fools we are, she thought, crossing Victoria Street.
For Heaven only knows why one loves it so, how one
sees it so, making it up, building it round one, tumbling it,
creating it every moment afresh; . . . In people's eyes,
in the swing, tramp, and trudge; in the bellow and the

uproar; the carriages, motor cars, omnibuses, vans, sandwich men shuffling and swinging; brass bands; barrel organs; in the triumph and the jingle and the strange high singing of some aeroplane overhead was what she loved; life; London; this moment of June.

As the 'centre of things' London, not surprisingly, inspired Virginia to write. She liked London for writing, she confided to her diary in 1924, 'partly because, as I say, life upholds one; and with my squirrel cage mind it's a great thing to be stopped circling. Then to see human beings freely and quickly is an infinite gain to me. And I can dart in and out and refresh my stagnancy'. London gave her not only the needed impetus and refreshment to write her books, it also gave her the subject-matter for them, as she realised: 'London itself perpetually attracts, stimulates, gives me a play and a story and a poem', she wrote in 1928, 'without any trouble, save that of moving my legs through the streets'. If she got stuck, as she frequently did with her novels, she would turn to London, 'seeing life, as I walk about the streets, an immense opaque block of material to be conveyed by me into its equivalent of language'. In a memorable phrase to Vita Sackville-West, she described these London walks as 'reviving my fires'.

If London stimulated Virginia's imagination, however, it also exhausted her with its too abundant 'life'. London seemed both necessary and destructive to her. For she was finely balanced between sanity and insanity and too much stimulus could bring on one of her breakdowns. So that, although she needed London to spark off ideas for new work, she also needed to migrate from London to carry out the actual writing of that work and to recover from the enormous imaginative effort it entailed.

In her intense response to London, Virginia stands with Dickens, Pepys, Johnson and Shakespeare. Indeed in what

she calls 'some odd corner of my dreaming mind' London
represents Dickens, Shakespeare and even Chaucer for
her, which is part of her 'passion for that great city'.
Sitting on a London bus, listening to a conversation
between a mother of eight children, a working-class intellectual and the bus-conductor, she concludes: 'This is
Dickens; or Shakespeare; or simple English cockney:
whichever it is I adore it; and warm the cockles of my
heart at it.'

On arriving back in central London after her only
prolonged absence from it, and misquoting enthusiastically
from William Dunbar, Virginia proclaims: 'London thou
art a jewel of jewels, and jasper of jocunditie — music, talk,
friendship, city views, books, publishing, something
central and inexplicable . . .' Starting with the 'music,
talk, friendship', this book will look first at her life, in
particular her response to the various houses in which she
lived and worked. In effect, this section will be a biographical sketch, with the emphasis on place and its impact
on Virginia. Her feelings of claustrophobia about her
Kensington birthplace give way to a sense of enormous
liberation when she moves with her sister and two brothers,
after the death of their father, to Bloomsbury. This in
turn changes to a feeling of bewilderment but also even
greater freedom when she moves with her brother Adrian,
after her sister's marriage, to two further Bloomsbury
houses. With her marriage to Leonard Woolf comes her
only prolonged absence from Bloomsbury and her attend-
ant sense of both relief and exile. Her move back to
Bloomsbury with Leonard in 1924 is accompanied with
great exhileration and a corresponding increase in creativity.
It is in this London house, between 1924 and 1939 that
Virginia is at her happiest and most productive. When
she leaves it for her last Bloomsbury house, which she
never really settles into, it is the end of London and the
end of her life. It is tempting to suggest that she could

not live without London. Since some of these London
houses no longer exist it seems particularly important
to try to bring them to life again. There will also be a
section on Virginia's country houses, which complement-
ed her London ones; Talland House, her childhood
holiday home in Cornwall, Asham and Monk's House,
her two main places of escape in adult life, and Charleston,
the house her sister Vanessa shared for many years with
Duncan Grant not far from Monk's House.

For any serious reader of Virginia Woolf the main
interest of her life lies in its relation to her work and it
is here that a study of Virginia Woolf's London offers
great interest. London is far more than a background to
her work, though it is that too. In almost every description
of London, Virginia uses it to reflect the inner world of
her characters, which absorbs her a great deal more than
the outer. In discarding such 'outer' elements of fiction
as elaborate plots, however, Virginia runs the risk of
incoherence and shapelessness and it is here that London
again comes to her aid. For she sees that it can help her
to shape and order her novels in a less obviously contrived
way than the conventional nineteenth-century 'plot'. At
times she also uses London to bring out the main themes
of the novel, particularly in *Mrs Dalloway* and *The Years*.
One of these themes is the effects of time: Big Ben
frequently reminds us in Virginia's work of the passage
of present time and many aspects of London are used
to remind us of its past history and pre-history. As we
have already seen, London is also used as a symbol of
'life', 'truth' or 'reality' in the novels. Perhaps the most
important role of London, however, is another aspect
already referred to—its ability to spark off Virginia's
poetic, at times even mystical vision, which is central to
her meaning. This 'vision' seems to depend on the bustle,
incongruity, even absurdity of London life. Held up by
the dancing and singing of a choir celebrating Lifeboat

Day in Trafalgar Square, Virginia can only say that she
'felt thrilled with an absurd visionary excitement; and
walked over Hungerford Bridge making up stories', though
she cannot explain why. This 'street frenzy', as she calls
it, has something 'courageous' about it, which she is forced
to admire more than the calm sublimity of Nature.

Virginia's intense 'vision' of London leads her to see
it at times not only as a symbol of 'life', but as symbolic
in all sorts of other ways, as the third section of this book
will show. Some of her symbolism is fairly obvious, as
when she uses Kensington to stand for social respectability,
Bloomsbury for bohemianism, Fleet Street and the City
for the world of business. However, London has changed
a great deal since Virginia's day, so that some of her
symbolism needs explaining. Chelsea, for Virginia, was a
place where a number of her aristocratic friends lived,
whereas it is today seen more in terms of bohemianism.
In fact, London has changed enormously in social terms.
It was very clearly a three class society at the beginning
of the twentieth century with each area having clearly
defined social connotations. Today it is much more of a
two class society with far greater social mobility. As a
result the areas where one may or may not live respectably
have become increasingly blurred. No one who aspired to
succeed socially in Virginia's day would have dared to live
in Camden Town or Hackney, for example, and most
districts south of the Thames were socially taboo. So
that when Virginia in *The Years* places the Pargiters'
eccentric cousin Sally in lodgings near Waterloo station
we are meant to understand just how little Sally cares for
social niceties. Very few of us, however, would be
ashamed of living in such an area today. Even London's
parks and squares have each their particular nuance for
Virginia and London monuments, such as Big Ben, St
Paul's and Westminster Abbey take on new shades of
meaning when viewed through her eyes. In other words,

there is as well-defined a Virginia Woolf's London as there is a Dickens's London which rewards examination both for its own sake and for the light it throws on her work.

Finally, for those who are not Londoners, and even for those who are, it seems very important that they should be able to explore the territory itself. One of Virginia's own 'greatest pleasures' was 'rambling the streets of London'. Like her father, she enjoyed the physical relief of walking offered from her mainly sedentary occupation. More than that, she could, like Keats's chameleon poet, enter into new experiences, at the same time escaping from herself. In an essay devoted entirely to 'Street-Haunting', she tries to explain her love of London's streets and their crowds:

> Into each of these lives one could penetrate a little way, far enough to give oneself the illusion that one is not tethered to a single mind, but can put on briefly for a few minutes the bodies and minds of others. One could become a washerwoman, a publican, a street singer. And what greater delight and wonder can there be than to leave the straight lines of personality and deviate into those footpaths that lead beneath brambles and thick tree trunks into the heart of the forest where live those wild beasts our fellow men?
>
> That is true: to escape is the greatest of pleasures; street-haunting in winter the greatest of adventures.

Paradoxically, the fiercer the London scene, the more refreshing Virginia finds it, as she confides to her diary: 'I walked along Oxford Street. The buses are strung on a chain. People fight and struggle. Knocking each other off the pavement. Old bareheaded men; a motor car accident; &c. To walk alone in London is the greatest rest.' As she grew older she depended more and more on her London

walks, which became her remedy for almost all ills. 'I'm
so ugly. So old,' she wrote in 1934. 'No one writes to
me. I'm . . . Well: don't think about it, and walk all over
London; and see people and imagine their lives'.

It is a pleasure to follow Virginia's favourite walks,
but it is also at times a help in understanding her work.
In walking from St James's to Regent's Park, for example,
in the footsteps of Clarissa Dalloway, Peter Walsh and
Septimus Smith, it is impossible to ignore the differences
between Clarissa's privileged territory of Belgravia and
Mayfair and Septimus's more proletarian background —
an important element in the theme of *Mrs Dalloway*.
Therefore, in order to help those who need it and to
interest those who enjoy following in her footsteps, a
number of walks round Virginia's London have been given
at the end, with maps included. There are also suggestions
for other trips to Richmond, Sussex and Cornwall for
those who may be interested.

1
A Biography of Place

In my experience what cuts the deepest channels in
our lives are the different houses in which we live —
deeper even than 'marriage and death and division',
so that perhaps the chapters of one's autobiography
should be determined by the different periods in which
one has lived in different houses . . . — Leonard Woolf,
Beginning Again

Virginia Woolf has a pronounced sense of place, which
emerges most clearly in her writing. Whilst trying
deliberately to get away from the detailed 'realism' of
many nineteenth century novelists, her works convey
an intense response to place. *Mrs Dalloway* and *The Years*,
for example, are as unmistakably London novels as
Dickens's *Oliver Twist* or *Little Dorritt*. Her sense of
place also figures strongly in her autobiographical writing
and it is this aspect that I want to explore first. Far more
has been written on Virginia's life than could possibly be
included here. By concentrating on her response to place,
particularly to London, I hope to bring out less familiar,
though no less illuminating aspects of both her life and
her writing.

22 Hyde Park Gate: Phase 1
(1882-1895)

Many of Virginia's earliest memories were of place. Looking back at the age of twenty-five, it seemed to her that
childhood had been divided into two large spaces: 'One
space was spent indoors in the drawing room and nursery,
and the other in Kensington Gardens'. Virginia had been
born and grew up in the highly respectable part of London

17

adjoining Kensington Gardens, an area she later came to despise though never entirely to escape. The first twenty-two years of her life were spent at 22 Hyde Park Gate, a long, narrow cul-de-sac slightly west of Queen's Gate facing Kensington Gardens. She retained a lasting impression of the street's narrowness, which enabled her to see a neighbour opposite washing her neck in her bedroom (just as Clarissa sees *her* neighbour preparing for bed at the end of *Mrs Dalloway*). As a result of this narrowness 22 Hyde Park Gate was rather dark, an effect emphasised by Virginia's mother's tastes. Julia Stephen, who had been brought up in the 'Watts-Venetian-Little Holland House' tradition, had covered the furniture in red velvet and painted the woodwork black with thin gold lines on it. (Later the thin gold lines were changed to raspberry ones and feature in Jacob's lodgings in *Jacob's Room*.) Virginia's sister, Vanessa, remembered how dark the rooms were, an effect which was exacerbated by a thick curtain of Virginia Creeper which hung over the back drawing room window. There was no electricity and the kitchen and other basement rooms could only be seen by candle- or lamp-light. The street outside the house was quiet, since very little came down the cul-de-sac, but inside it must have been rather noisy. For here eight children, their parents and six or seven servants lived in small bedrooms with one bathroom and three water-closets between them. To house them all Virginia's parents had felt it necessary to add two storeys and at least one back addition to the house. This was carried out in a rather random fashion from plans sketched by her mother, to save architect's fees. The result was a high, narrow house with a Dutch gable top, divided into numerous, small, oddly-shaped rooms.

This large household had come into being through the previous marriages of both Virginia's parents. Her father, Leslie Stephen, had first married the daughter of

1. *22 Hyde Park Gate, Kensington*: Virginia's birthplace and family home.

William Thackeray, Harriet (known as 'Minny') and they
had had one daughter, Laura, in 1870. Even before
Minny's death in 1875 it had become plain that Laura
was a backward child. By the time she reached her teens
Virginia remembered her as a vacant-eyed girl whose
idiocy was becoming daily more obvious, who could
hardly read, who would throw the scissors into the fire,
who was tongue-tied and stammered and yet had to appear
at table with the rest of them. It was not until Laura was
twenty-one that she was put in an asylum, where she
survived Virginia, not dying until 1945. The second
strand of the family came from Virginia's mother, Julia's,
first marriage. Julia, born Jackson in 1846, had married
a handsome young barrister, Herbert Duckworth, in
1867. Three years later, when she was only twenty-four,
he died, leaving her with three children: George, born in
1868, Stella, born in 1869, and Gerald, born after his
father's death in 1870. Julia had been a widow for eight
years and Leslie a widower for three when they married
in 1878. Four more children followed, only two of them
intended: Vanessa in 1879, Thoby in 1880, and then the
two 'mistakes', Virginia in 1882, and Adrian in 1883.

Like the Ramsays in Virginia's highly autobiographical
To the Lighthouse, Leslie and Julia had eight children
between them. It was no wonder Virginia felt that 22
Hyde Park Gate was bursting at the seams. The basement
was given over to the cook, Sophy Farrell, and other
servants and the ground floor to the family, who lived
and entertained in a large double room, with a dining-
room off it. On the first floor was Leslie and Julia's bedroom with a nursery next door for the children when
they were very small. Above that were three bedrooms
for the growing Duckworths, George, Stella and Gerald,
and on the third floor a day and a night nursery for the
Stephen children as they got beyond the baby stage. At
the top of the house, in a large, airy room, their father

who was a scholar and man of letters, worked at his
books in a well-stocked library, which was to form the
main source of Virginia's education. When lying in bed
at night the children would often hear the thud of Leslie's
books hitting the floor above them. It was an early
introduction to the world of literature.

Number 22 was a lively place. In addition to their own
large family, the Stephens constantly entertained a series
of aunts, uncles and cousins. In all, Virginia had twenty-
three cousins, a number of whom took up important
positions in public life. She herself best describes her background:

> Who was I then? Adeline Virginia Stephen, the second
> daughter of Leslie and Julia Prinsep Stephen, born
> on 25th January 1882, descended from a great many
> people, some famous, others obscure; born into a
> large connection, born not of rich parents, but of well-
> to-do parents, born into a very communicative, literate,
> letterwriting, visiting, articulate, late nineteenth century
> world . . .

The centre of this world for Virginia, as a child, was
undoubtedly her mother. One of her earliest memories
was of 'red and purple flowers on a black ground—my
mother's dress; and she was sitting either in a train or in
an omnibus, and I was on her lap'. Virginia was obsessed
by her mother until the age of forty, when she wrote her
out of her system by portraying her as Mrs Ramsay in
To the Lighthouse.

Julia was born a Jackson, but the more interesting side
to her background lay with her mother, Maria Pattle.
Maria's mother, a Frenchwoman Adeline de L'Etang,
had been born in India and there made an unfortunate
marriage to a James Pattle. After his death, she came to
London with her seven daughters, and the 'Pattle sisters',

as they were known, became famous for their beauty
and talent. Apart from Julia's mother, Maria, there was
Virginia, who married an earl, Julia [Cameron] who
became famous as a photographer, and Sara, who married
an Anglo-Indian administrator. When Sara eventually
returned to England with her husband, Thoby Prinsep,
she set up an informal 'salon' at Little Holland House.
Here she entertained many famous writers, politicians
and painters, including Tennyson, Thackeray, Disraeli,
Gladstone, Watts, Holman-Hunt, Burne-Jones and
Ruskin.

Julia spent a great deal of time as a child at her aunt's
house in Holland Park, partly, Virginia suspected,
because her beauty made her welcome to the painters.
It may have been here that she acquired her love of
literature, particularly Scott, for whom she had a passion.
It was certainly here that she learnt to appreciate culture
and intellect to a degree unusual for a woman of her
time. Indeed, she fell in love with Leslie Stephen's work
before she grew to love him! Virginia attributed what she
called her 'romanticism' to her mother's family: 'I think
it must have been my Great Aunts,' she told Lytton
Strachey, with a certain amount of pride.

Yet Julia herself was not what one might call a
'romantic'—not at any rate by the time Virginia was
born. She had, it is true, made a first romantic marriage
to dashing young Herbert Duckworth, with whom she
fell madly in love in Venice at the age of twenty-one.
Three years later, however, with his early and unexpected
death, she had been forced to come to terms with the
grim reality of bringing up three small children alone. By
the time she married Leslie Stephen, eight years later,
she had few romantic illusions left and those few were
severely taxed. For, though Julia adored Leslie and he
her, he was an extremely difficult, demanding man with
a retarded daughter into the bargain. After four more

children Julia must have found life even more trying, particularly since she was always ready to help anyone in need. Yet she was by no means the saint Leslie afterwards made her out to be. Like Mrs Ramsay, she had her faults, especially that of trying to arrange other people's lives. She also had a strong sense of humour, which could be quite satirical, even in relation to her venerable husband. (He was fifteen years her senior and a well-known scholar by the time they married.) Virginia remembered her as 'the most prompt, practical and vivid of human beings', whose 'amazing sense of life' ensured that even 'that interminable and incongruous procession, which is the life of a large family, went merrily'. She saw both determination and melancholy in her mother's face, the first urging her to activity, but the second very conscious of the uselessness of that activity. This gave her beauty and femininity a certain dignity, even austerity which made her, again like Mrs Ramsay, seem rather remote at times.

Julia was, however, less remote from her children than many women of her age and class, for she insisted on giving them their primary education herself, apart from mathematics, which Leslie undertook. Before Virginia was seven Julia was trying to teach her Latin, History and French. She was not very successful. The only advantage Virginia could find in the arrangement was the establishment of a very close, if trying, relationship with her mother and a rapid knowledge of her true nature.

Schooling took place in the day nursery on the third floor, where the four Stephen children also had their meals. The nursery table seemed huge to Virginia as a child, particularly the space beneath it, where she would hide with Vanessa and exchange childish questions. The night nursery Virginia recalled as equally vast and, in addition, frightening at times. For in winter there would be a fire, which terrified Virginia if it burnt after she

went to bed. She had many arguments with Adrian, who
liked the flames and refused to have them extinguished,
but agreed to Nurse's compromise of a towel folded over
the fender. Virginia lost her fear of the fire only after
Thoby had left for school. By then she and Vanessa had
started to tell each other stories about their neighbours,
the Dilke family, which probably distracted her attention.

Kensington Gardens also seemed vast to Virginia as a
child. The young Stephens' day had a strict routine,
which included two walks to the conveniently close park.
Their nearest entrance was Queen's Gate, where they
would pass a thin old lady selling nuts and bootlaces.
Virginia preferred the longer way round, through
Gloucester Gate, because she was fascinated by the fat
old lady who sat there with a huge bunch of balloons.
When she was allowed a penny to buy one of these red
or purple wonders, she would dance away with it in
rapture. Once inside Kensington Gardens the walks varied
slightly, but usually involved going up the Broad Walk,
or along the Flower Walk to the Round Pond. Virginia
remembered these walks as dull, but nevertheless recalled
them in vivid detail, especially in her novels, which help
us to visualize her there. In the 1891 section of *The Years*
(when Virginia would have been nine) Morris Pargiter
shuffles his feet through the dry leaves in the Law
Courts remembering his childhood: 'Not yet trodden
down the leaves lay in Kensington Gardens, and children,
crunching the shells as they ran, scooped up a handful
and scudded on through the mist down the avenues, with
their hoops'. Every autumn, as the Stephen children
returned to their daily routine, after several months'
break, they always abused the Broad Walk for only
pretending to be a hill. As the weeks passed, however, it
seemed to them steeper and steeper, until by the time
they were ready to leave for their summer holidays it
had become a proper hill again. Virginia and Adrian

found the Flower Walk particularly exciting, since Vanessa and Thoby claimed that there was once a real swamp behind it, where they had found the skeleton of a dog. It was the Round Pond, however, that provided most entertainment, whether it was sailing their boats there or, in very severe winters, skating on it. A description in another section of *The Years* brings back the scene almost more vividly than an actual visit:

> It was admirably composed. There was the white figure of Queen Victoria against a green bank; beyond, was the red brick of the old palace; the phantom Church raised its spire, and the Round Pond made a pool of blue. A race of yachts was going forward. The boats leant on their sides so that the sails touched the water. There was a nice little breeze.

Other events helped break up what Virginia called 'the eternal round of Kensington Gardens'. Sometimes the children were allowed to buy sweets at the white house near the palace; once a week they bought the magazine, *Tit-Bits*, to which Virginia unsuccessfully contributed a story; at other times they raced their go-carts, not very skilfully, and annoyed old ladies. In winter, when their choice was more limited, they told each other an endless saga—the Jim Joe and Harry Hoe story—about three brothers who had herds of animals and adventures.

Neither the stories nor the activities could compete in Virginia's mind with those of her summer holidays at Talland House in Cornwall.* Leslie Stephen had discovered the house in 1881, the year before Virginia's birth. He had been on one of his many walking tours when he came across St Ives, 'at the very toenail,' as he put it, 'of England'. Virginia's first summer must, therefore, have been spent, as the following twelve were, in the large

*See page 219.

shabby house overlooking Carbis Bay. (The same house
served as a model for the Ramsays' holiday home in *To
the Lighthouse*.) It is no wonder Kensington Gardens,
which she associated mainly with the constraints of
winter, seemed dull by comparison.

Both Talland House and, to a large extent, childhood
were brought to an abrupt end by one of the greatest
disasters of Virginia's life—her mother's death.

Julia, whom everyone agreed 'did too much', was
only forty-nine when she died on 5 May 1895, after a
brief illness diagnosed as influenza. Virginia was just
thirteen and Vanessa, the eldest Stephen child, not quite
sixteen. The effects on Virginia are incalculable, but it
is quite clear that shortly after her mother's death she
became mentally disturbed, so much so that the family
doctor, Dr Seton, prescribed a strict régime of outdoor
exercise and no lessons. She did, however, continue to
read compulsively, though she lost her usual desire to
write. In addition, she became highly self-critical and
extremely irritable.

22 Hyde Park Gate: Phase 2
(1895-1904)

Leslie Stephen also reacted violently to Julia's death,
though his grief took the form of terrible groans and
passionate lamentations, reminiscent of a Hebrew
prophet. In his 'Oriental gloom', Virginia tells us, it was
Stella Duckworth, Julia's eldest daughter of twenty-six,
on whom he leant most heavily. Besides listening to her
step-father endlessly bemoaning his failure to tell Julia
how much he had loved her, Stella would also provide
him with constant distractions to help him through the
day. On a practical level she took over the running of the
large household and the upbringing of the Stephen child-

ren. Stella had been almost morbidly close to her mother
and had waited on her every need. When Virginia, at the
age of six or seven, needed to be chaperoned around
London, Stella would undertake it, not forgetting to give
her milk and biscuits in a tea-shop on the way. Stella had
a strong sense of inferiority, particularly to her mother,
but also to Leslie Stephen with his fierce intellectuality.
For Stella was not clever and seldom read a book. However, Virginia felt that she did have character, though not
perhaps in the usual sense of the word, being 'very gentle,
very honest and in some way individual'. Partly as a
result of this modesty and honesty, which showed itself
in her lack of pose or snobbery, she had great charm. It
was Stella's genuineness, her 'sensitiveness to real things',
which distinguished her from her brothers, whom
Virginia found 'so opaque and conventional', full of
'shrewd middle-class complacence and instinctive
worldliness'. Presumably Stella had inherited her mother's
sensibilities rather than what Virginia called 'Duckworth
philistinism'.

As Virginia grew up she was aware that Stella's quiet
beauty had attracted a number of suitors, in particular a
respectable young solicitor, John ('Jack') Waller Hills. It
was not until her mother died, however, that Stella
finally agreed to marry Jack. Whether it was from apathy
or from a subconscious wish to escape her step-father's
incessant emotional demands is not clear. What is quite
plain is that once married and out of the gloomy
atmosphere of 22 Hyde Park Gate, Stella bloomed. It
was a brief happiness, for within three months of her
wedding, and only two years after her mother, Stella too
had died, of peritonitis.

This time the immediate crisis in the Stephen household was not so great, since Vanessa had already taken
on many of Stella's responsibilities. On her marriage in
April 1897 Stella had moved into her own house, though

it was only a few doors away to make Leslie feel less abandoned. Virginia believed that, apart from Jack, Vanessa had suffered most by Stella's death. She herself seems to have reacted most violently to Stella's marriage and subsequent illness. Her nervous instability had become so pronounced by May 1897 that Dr Seton once more ordered milk, outdoor exercise and no lessons. There is little doubt that when Stella left 22 Hyde Park Gate in April 1897 Virginia felt that even her substitute mother was being taken away from her. When Stella became ill, Virginia herself grew feverish. Curiously enough, Stella's actual death affected Virginia less and her health began to improve.

Nevertheless, Virginia was left once again without a mother-figure and it is not surprising that she turned to Vanessa for consolation. For Vanessa was the more practical, the more solid, the earthier and the elder of the two sisters. Virginia clung to her for the rest of her life, even after she was happily married herself, obviously placing her in the role of a mother. As late as 1921 she was asking Vanessa, only half-jokingly, 'why did you bring me into the world to go through these ordeals?' On another occasion she wrote: 'Where should I have been if it hadn't been for you, when Hyde Park Gate was at its worst? You must admit the Apes [one of Virginia's nicknames as a child, the other was Billygoat] were a fair handful in those days'. At times Virginia seems almost incestuously close to Vanessa, wanting to kiss her all over and extravagantly admiring her beauty. At the age of fifty-five she told Vanessa that she had been 'in love with her ever since I was a green-eyed brat under the nursery table'. She herself recognised that she was 'more nearly attached to Vanessa than sisters should be'. Vanessa was always for Virginia, her 'lovely Dolphin, with the spangled tail, the sea-blue eyes, and the heart of a fish'. The last phrase implies that Virginia often felt that Vanessa did not return her love as warmly as she might; she contrasted her overflowing affection to Vanessa's 'thimbleful'. The first phrase, 'lovely Dolphin', reveals Virginia's tendency to cast those she loved and herself in the guise of fish, birds or animals. To her family Virginia was always 'the Apes' or 'Billygoat', to her husband 'Mandril', to another close friend 'Sparroy' (i.e. Sparrow). They in turn became 'Mongoose' or 'Dolphin'. These nicknames made a point in a humorous way. In Vanessa's case, the dolphin stood for a beautiful, but wild, creature, with a cold heart. Yet Vanessa herself was as capable of deep affection as Virginia, only she showed it less. Her daughter wrote of her:

Vanessa had a kind of stoical warmth about her, a monolithic quality that reminded one now of the implacable smile of primitive Aphrodite, now of the hollow wind-whistling statues of Erewhon. She sat and sewed or painted or listened; she was always sitting, sometimes at the head of the table, sometimes by the fire, sometimes under the apple tree. Even if she said little, there emanated from her an enormous power, a pungency like the smell of crushed sage. She presided, wise yet diffident, affectionate and a little remote, full of unquenchable spirit. Her feelings were strong, and words seemed to her inadequate.

Virginia was undoubtedly jealous of Vanessa's strengths, particularly when she went on to have children. Vanessa seemed to her so solid and confident, a mother-earth figure surrounded by over-abundance of life, while she, Virginia, struggled on precariously in virtual isolation.

At 22 Hyde Park Gate, however, it was Vanessa's stubborn independence which struck Virginia, especially in her dealings with their father. Leslie had a quite un-founded fear of losing all his money and kept a very close eye on the weekly accounts. When he went into one of his recurring rages with Vanessa over the amount spent, instead of bursting into tears, as Stella would have done, she, to his further fury, remained totally unmoved. This weekly scene with Vanessa contributed to the children's picture of their father at this time as 'a tyrant of inconceivable selfishness, who had replaced the beauty and merriment of the dead with ugliness and gloom'.

Leslie Stephen's temper had not been improved by his insistence on taking up the children's education after Julia's death. Thoby had already left for Clifton College and Adrian attended his prep. school, Evelyns, but the girls remained at home to suffer the impatience of their father. In theory Leslie believed in the importance of education for women. In practise he largely observed the conventions of the time which dictated that far more money and care were spent on boys than on girls. Virginia was afterwards resentful that all the family funds went on giving the boys a 'good' education, whilst she and Vanessa were left to the mercies of their father and miscellaneous tutors. Leslie soon tired of trying to teach them and handed them over to other teachers. Some of them were very good, others less so. Vanessa, who showed a strong interest in art, learnt a great deal from her drawing-master, Ebenezer Cook, and Virginia, who was more interested in language, began to enjoy Greek with her tutor, Janet Case. Janet, who was to remain a life-long friend, had replaced Clara Pater, the sister of Walter Pater.

Neither Virginia nor Vanessa enjoyed their dancing, deportment or music lessons, though they quite liked singing lessons. Both had their own passionate interest, in Vanessa's case, painting and drawing, in Virginia's, reading and writing. Vanessa taught herself a great deal by working through Ruskin's *The Elements of Drawing*, while Virginia devoured most of her father's large library without any of the usual strict censorship common at the time. Leslie Stephen would also bring her books from the London Library. In many ways Virginia appreciated her lack of formal education, but in others regretted it. She agreed with a friend who later argued that she had escaped the 'jolly vulgarity' of girls' schools: 'But then think how I was brought up! No school; mooning about alone among my father's books; never any chance to pick up all that goes on in schools—throwing balls; ragging; slang; vulgarity; scenes; jealousies—only rages with my half brothers, and being walked off my feet round the Serpentine by my father'. Most of her life Virginia felt cut off from ordinary people and the feeling began in childhood.

Virginia had already started writing seriously at the age of nine, when she founded a small family paper, *The Hyde Park Gate News*, which she kept up weekly until 1895. At fifteen or sixteen, inspired by such Elizabethan writers as Hakluyt, she began writing a long, picturesque novel upon the Christian religion, called *Religio Laici*, proving that man has need of a God, but the God was described in the process of change. Her feminist sympathies found early expression in a history of women and she also wrote a history of her own family—'all very long-winded and Elizabethan in style'. Though her mother's death and her own mental illness had put a stop to her writing for a time, it was only a brief period. She continued to write compulsively all her life, whether it was fiction, essays, reviews, diaries or letters, and was miserable whenever she was ordered, for reasons of health, to stop.

As the Stephen children grew up, not only the daily routine changed, but also the lay-out of the house. Each child was given its own bed-sitting room, sometimes by dividing one large room into two, and the day nursery on the third floor became a studio for Virginia and

Vanessa. Apart from the hours Vanessa had begun to spend at the Academy art school, they would pass most of their time together there. They were now the only two females left in a household of six males, and they instinctively banded together in a conspiracy. Since they respected neither Aunt Mary, Julia's married sister, nor Aunt Minnie, Julia's unmarried sister-in-law, both of whom were anxious to 'help', there seemed no one else to turn to but each other. Though Virginia had been very jealous of her elder sister in childhood, taunting her with devastating articulateness and nicknaming her 'the saint', she now got on much better with her. A typical day would be one spent together with only their father shut safely in his study. In the evening Adrian would come back from Westminster School, which he attended as a day-boy. Jack Hills, who spent most of his time with them, would follow from Lincoln's Inn, then Gerald from J.M. Dent's publishing house and finally George from the Treasury where he worked. Thoby would be at Clifton, later at Cambridge. Virginia saw life at 22 Hyde Park Gate round about 1900 as a complete model of Victorian society. The day would start with a family breakfast at 8.30 a.m., when either she or Vanessa would be present to watch Adrian bolt his food and rush off to school. Leslie would appear next, followed by George and Gerald. Once Vanessa had ordered dinner from Sophy, the Stephens' faithful cook, she would dash off to catch a bus to the Academy, unless Gerald was ready and offered to take her in his daily hansom cab. George spent longer over his breakfast, sometimes persuading Virginia to sit down while he related gossip from the previous night's party. However, he would eventually leave for the Treasury, always immaculately dressed. Alone in the house, except for her father, Sophy and a few maids, Virginia would go up to her own room to study Greek, in preparation for her twice-weekly lesson

with Janet Case. For three whole hours Virginia felt
that both she and Vanessa escaped the pressure of
Victorian society, meeting again at lunch, then spending
another few hours more or less as they chose. By 4.30,
however, society began to exert its pressure, for they
must be 'in' to receive visitors, and at 5 the visitors and
their father must be given tea. Virginia thought of these
occasions as a game with elaborate rules which had, painfully, to be learnt. Years afterwards she still found herself
playing this game, for she saw that, in spite of its artificial-
ity, it had its uses and its beauty, based on restraint,
sympathy and unselfishness. Yet her attitude throughout
her life was highly ambivalent. On the one hand she
wanted to, and did, cast off the conventions of her childhood; on the other she remained fascinated by 'society'
and all its rituals.

One of the most important rituals at 22 Hyde Park
Gate was dressing for dinner at 7.30 a.m. Since they were
children the Stephens had participated, meeting such
illustrious friends of Leslie's as George Meredith, Henry
James, Mrs Humphrey Ward, Herbert Spencer, John
Addington Symonds and James Russell Lowell, who
was Virginia's godfather. Through their mother's connect-
ion with her aunt Sara Prinsep and Little Holland House,
they also saw at family dinners artists like Watts, Burne-
Jones and Leighton. Dressing for dinner was, understandably, an important business. However cold or foggy the
weather, once Virginia and Vanessa had reached their
teens, they were expected to appear at 8 in evening dress,
with arms and neck bare. Virginia earned George's
eternal disapproval by appearing at one dinner in a green
dress, made of cheap furnishing material in an attempt
to economise. (Her allowance was £50 a year and a
house dress usually cost a few pounds, whilst a party
dress cost fifteen guineas, if made by their dressmaker,
Mrs Young.) George, who was the soul of convention,

ordered her peevishly to 'go and tear it up', though
Gerald, to Virginia's gratitude, said he rather liked it.

This was only one of many occasions on which George
made Virginia extremely unhappy. Like Hugh Whitbread
in *Mrs Dalloway*, who is based on George, he was totally
committed to the social game. This may have been partly
due to the fact that he had failed in his attempt to
become a diplomat. Whatever the reason, Virginia insisted
that he had learnt the rules of that game so well that he
emerged at the age of sixty with a knighthood, an
aristocratic wife, a sinecure, a large country house and
three sons. (The last seems somewhat irrelevant!) Meantime, in the early nineteen hundreds, she and Vanessa,
in the absence of their mother, must be made by George
to play that game too. Vanessa had just 'come out' by
the time Stella died in 1897, but there was still Virginia
to introduce to what she regarded as the tortures of
society. After Vanessa had finally refused to accompany
George to one more dance or party, he fastened on
Virginia, who found the whole business of trying to make
polite conversation and get partners for the dances both
frustrating and humiliating. Nevertheless, as a budding
novelist and social observer, she drew consolation from
what she called 'the scene as spectacle to be described
later'. George, who sensed both his step-sisters' rebel-
liousness even before it was expressed, only increased his
efforts to launch them into high society.

The worst aspect of Virginia's outings with George,
however, was the return. She would no sooner undress
and get into bed, than George would creep in and fling
himself at her. What would the old ladies of Kensington
and Belgravia, who admired George's almost parental
care, have thought, Virginia wondered, if they had known
he was her 'lover' too? What exactly she meant by 'lover'
is not clear. George did, undeniably, make sexual
approaches to her, for her doctor attributed one of her

nervous breakdowns to them. These semi-incestuous fumblings may also help to explain her sexual frigidity in later life. On the other hand, they must not be exaggerated, for Virginia herself said that when George eventually married he was still a virgin.

George told the family doctor that he kissed and cuddled his step-sister in order to comfort her for the fatal illness of her father. This must have been in 1903, when Virginia was twenty-one and Leslie was known to be dying of cancer of the stomach. He had been told of the cancer in spring 1902 and had been operated on in December. He lingered on through 1903 into February 1904, a period which was even gloomier and more limited socially for the Stephen sisters than their already rather restricted life. When their father eventually died, it was in some ways a relief.

In the same year that Leslie discovered he had cancer he was also offered a knighthood for his services to literature, which he accepted only under pressure. These 'services' included the editorship of *The Cornhill Magazine* from 1871 to 1882 and the even more prestigious and certainly more monumental *Dictionary of National Biography* from 1882 to 1891. His many works of literary criticism, history and philosophy were centred on the eighteenth century, which helps to explain Virginia's own love of the period. She greatly admired her father's critical works for their perception, clarity and conciseness, which illustrated the Cambridge analytical spirit at its best. His 'creative' powers she found less successful: 'give him life, a character, and he is so crude, so elementary, so conventional, that a child with a box of coloured chalks is as subtle a portrait painter as he is'. This she attributed to the crippling effect of a one-sided education and a lifetime of intensive brain work unrelieved by any outside interests, such as art, music, theatre or travel.

Both Leslie's background and upbringing make it easy to see why, at the age of sixty-five, Virginia could describe him in these terms. He came from a mixed background of farmers, merchants, smugglers, but predominantly lawyers. As far back as Leslie's great-grandfather, the Stephen men had been writers, many of them polemicists. Grandfather James was a fierce opponent of slavery and eventually married a member of the Clapham Sect, Jane Venn. The Clapham Sect was an evangelical group greatly concerned about slavery, as well as missionary work. Above all they cared for justice. Leslie's father was naturally attracted to the Law as the theoretical arbiter of Justice. Having started his career in law, however, he eventually moved to the Colonial Office, where he felt he could best carry on the family fight against slavery. Leslie seems to have inherited not only his father's strong sense of justice, but also its reverse side, his implacability. At times this led Virginia to call her father brutal, even tyrannical, particularly in his treatment of women and children. A more attractive feature of both father and son was their extreme industriousness, which was almost certainly linked to their strong puritanism. For, though Leslie lost his faith quite early in life, he remained basically committed to the evangelical principles of hard work and moral uprightness. Yet with all his abilities and achievements he was, like his father, basically vulnerable, shy and deeply pessimistic — a 'skinless' man, as he himself put it. A nervous, over-sensitive child, he had found Eton a terrifying place, only made bearable by the protection of his older, tougher brother, Fitzjames. Cambridge had been less traumatic, partly because by this time Leslie had, in self-defence, taken up sport. In his determination not to be weak, he became surprisingly athletic, renowned for his rowing, walking and mountaineering, all sports which require determination rather than pure physical

strength. Virginia grew up, she told a friend, with alpen-
stocks in her nursery and a raised map of the Alps
showing every peak her father had climbed. By the time
she was born his mountaineering days were over, but he
still went on long walking tours, as his discovery of
Talland House in 1881 shows. Virginia attributed her
own need to walk at least two hours daily, whether in
the town or country, to her father's example — 'only he
would have gone a whole day with a tin box of sandwiches,
carefully packed by my mother'.

At Cambridge Leslie had taken up teaching, in the
absence of any other interests it would seem. He gained a
Fellowship at Trinity Hall, which involved taking Holy
Orders. He was therefore ordained in 1859, the same year
that his father died. It was perhaps the knowledge that
his father could no longer be hurt by his growing disbelief
that enabled him publicly to declare it and, as a con-
sequence, abandon his Fellowship.

Leaving Cambridge for London, he began to make a
name for himself, first as a journalist, then as a literary
critic. The character of Mr Ramsay in *To the Lighthouse*,
which Virginia based almost entirely on her father, highlights Leslie's interest in philosophy. It also shows his
sense of failure in this area, which Virginia attributed to
his more endearing qualities. Had he not burdened himself with eight children, or been less involved with them,
she suggests, he might have succeeded in the abstract
world of philosophy. The most attractive side of Leslie,
however, was precisely the ability to become involved,
particularly with small children. Virginia remembered
him mending her toy boat one evening at 22 Hyde Park
Gate 'and how interested he became and said, with his
little snort, half-laughing, something like "Absurd — what
fun it is doing this". Beautiful he was at such moments,'
she said, 'simple and eager as a child; and exquisitely alive
to all affection; exquisitely tender'.

Leslie seems then to have been an impossible mixture
of harshness and sensitivity, the one always trying to
compensate for the other. His strong sense of failure
and self-pity made Virginia hate him at times as a child,
but as she grew up she began to realise how much more
she preferred his world, symbolised by his study full of
books, to the social world of George Duckworth, symbolised by the drawing-room below. On many occasions,
going to change a book in Leslie's study, she was struck
by the sharp division in her life:

> There I would find him, swinging in his rocking chair,
> pipe in mouth. Slowly he would realize my presence.
> Rising, he would go to the shelves, put the book back
> and very kindly ask me what I had made of it? Perhaps
> I was reading Johnson. For some time we would talk
> and then, feeling soothed, stimulated, full of love for
> this unworldly, very distinguished, lonely man, I would
> go down to the drawing room again and hear George's
> patter. There was no connection.

Though she adored her mother as a child, at the age of
six Virginia told Vanessa that she preferred her father.
No doubt she could identify with him more, not only
with his literary interests but also with his temperament.
'We Stephens,' she told a friend in 1924, 'are difficult,
especially as the race tapers out, towards its finish —
such cold fingers, so fastidious, so critical, such taste'.
Of all Leslie's children she was the closest, devouring all
the books he humped back for her from the London
Library, talking to him shyly about her tastes in literature
and going for long walks with him round the Serpentine.
He was particularly proud of her literary talent. When,
as a child, she demanded yet another volume of whatever
she was reading, perhaps Gibbon, Spedding, Bacon or
Cowper, he would say, proudly, 'Gracious, child, how

you gobble!' At the risk of sounding sentimental she
described him as 'an adorable man, and somehow
tremendous'. Though she found him fierce and intoler-
able at times, she mainly remembered him as disinterested,
high-minded and tender, to her at least. In his last illness
they grew even closer.

So that when Leslie eventually died on 22 February
1904, Virginia felt his death most strongly. She reacted
violently, entering into her worst mental breakdown yet.
By May she had begun to hear voices, tried to starve herself and became physically violent. Vanessa, whom
Virginia now regarded with deepest suspicion, had to
hire three nurses to look after her. The greatest support,
however, came from Virginia's close friend at that time,
Violet Dickinson. Violet, who had aristocratic connections, had been a particular friend of Stella's, and to some
extent replaced Stella for Virginia after Stella's death.
Virginia also developed an intense passion for her, of the
kind she had suffered for her cousin by marriage, Madge
Vaughan, in the middle and late 1890s. Madge Symonds,
the daughter of John Addington Symonds, had been
brought up in Switzerland in a much freer atmosphere
than the Stephen girls and seemed to them, particularly
after the tragic death of her father in 1893, a highly
romantic figure. Virginia's passionate feelings for her
are vividly expressed in Clarissa Dalloway's youthful
worship of Sally Seton. Once Madge had married
Virginia's cousin, William Vaughan, in 1898, and left
for Yorkshire, Virginia's passion inevitably abated, so
that when Violet joined the Stephens on holiday at
Fritham in the New Forest in 1902, Virginia was ready
to fall in love again. Though not physically attractive
and well above average height, Violet dressed well.
Whether she wore flowing, picturesque evening gowns,
or smart blue serge suits with fashionably short skirts,
Virginia found her striking, in spite of her rather comical

face. What she admired, and needed most, however, was Violet's cheerful and outgoing manner. She loved the way Violet entered into whatever was going on, 'with a most youthful zeal', though eighteen years Virginia's senior. Violet also encouraged Virginia to believe in herself as a writer. So that, when Leslie Stephen died and Virginia's health broke down, Violet's offer of help was gladly accepted. She took Virginia off to the house she shared with her brother at Burnham Wood. During her three months there Virginia tried to commit suicide by throwing herself from a window, the fate she ordains for Septimus in *Mrs Dalloway*. Like Septimus, too, she heard the birds talking Greek, and, unlike Septimus, she also heard King Edward VII swearing foully in the azalea bushes outside her window.

By September, when she joined Vanessa and her brothers on their summer holidays at the Manor House, Teversal, Nottinghamshire, Virginia was better but by no means fully recovered. So that when the Stephens finally started to move from Hyde Park Gate to Bloomsbury at the end of 1904, Virginia was sent away again. First she stayed with her father's unmarried sister, Caroline Emelia in Cambridge, then with her first love, Madge Vaughan, at her husband's school, Giggleswick, in Yorkshire. The move from Hyde Park Gate had already been agreed on before Leslie's death. In fact it was one of the more positive aspects of it. For all four children felt the need to free themselves from what they had come to regard as the oppressive 'social' life of Kensington.

46 Gordon Square (1905-1907)

Vanessa had chosen Bloomsbury because of its distance from Kensington and all it stood for. Bloomsbury was not nearly so respectable socially, as the Stephens' friends and relations immediately indicated. In fact Bloomsbury could even have been described as Bohemian, a place where students of London University and the Slade School of Art took lodgings, not to mention the artists' 'models' and other dubious types. The convenience of the Slade had probably influenced Vanessa's choice, as well as the even more practical aspect of lower rents. Though Leslie had left his children £15,000 each, about £350,000 by today's values, they were none of them actually earning money, so felt they had to be careful with it. Virginia saw the move in symbolic terms, a 'curious transition from tyranny to freedom'. She recognised that Gordon Square, where they rented number 46, was not one of the most romantic of the Bloomsbury squares, yet she found it in 1904 the most beautiful, exciting and romantic place imaginable:

> To begin with it was astonishing to stand at the drawing room window and look into all those trees . . . instead of looking at old Mrs Redgrave washing her neck across the way. The light and the air after the rich red gloom of Hyde Park Gate were a revelation. Things one had never seen in the darkness there — Watts pictures, Dutch cabinets, blue china — shone out for the first time in the drawing room at Gordon Square. After the muffled silence of Hyde Park Gate the roar of traffic was positively alarming. Odd characters, sinister, strange, prowled and slunk past our windows. But what was even more exhilarating was the extraordinary increase of space. At Hyde Park Gate one had only a bedroom in which to read or see one's friends. Here Vanessa and I each had a sitting room; and a study on the ground floor. To make it all newer and fresher, the house had been completely done up. Needless to say the Watts-Venetian tradition

2. *46 Gordon Square, Bloomsbury*: the house Virginia shared
with Thoby, Vanessa and
Adrian Stephen after their
father's death in 1904.

of red plush and black paint had been reversed; we
had entered the Sargent-Furse era; white and green
chintzes were everywhere; and instead of Morris wall-
papers with their intricate patterns we decorated our
walls with washes of plain distemper. We were full of
experiments and reforms. We were going to do without
table napkins, . . . we were going to paint; to write;
to have coffee after dinner instead of tea at nine
o'clock. Everything was going to be new; everything
was going to be different. Everything was on trial.

46 Gordon Square was and still is typical of Bloomsbury. One of a terrace of early Victorian houses, it consists
of a rendered basement and ground floor, balconied first
floor and three further storeys of diminishing elegance.
Sophy Farrell's kitchen and the servants' room were in
the basement, the dining-room, living-room and library,
used as Thoby's study, on the ground floor, the double
L-shaped drawing room with communicating doors on
the first floor and the four bedrooms and individual
sitting-rooms on the second, third and fourth floors.
Vanessa had bought a new desk and sofa for Virginia's
sitting-room, which was at the very top of the house.
Here, *standing* at her desk, in emulation of Vanessa standing at her easel, she would work for hours. She was still
writing compulsively and had at last had an article
accepted by a weekly newspaper, *The Guardian*. In
addition she was helping Frederic Maitland with a
biography of her father. Another two or three years were
to pass before she made a serious attempt at a novel, and
another ten before that first novel was published as *The
Voyage Out* in 1915. Soon after her arrival in Gordon
Square she also took up quite a different occupation, as
a part-time teacher at Morley College, an evening institute
for working men and women in the Waterloo Road. The
Principal, Miss Sheepshanks, a daughter of the Bishop of

Norwich, initially persuaded Virginia to give some 'talks' about books and pictures, but in time Virginia found herself trying to teach English History and English Composition. She carried on teaching at Morley until 1907, in spite of the discouragement she felt at the low standards of the students and her depression at their general deprivation.

Meantime Virginia enjoyed life at Gordon Square immensely, not least because it differed so entirely from 22 Hyde Park Gate. To be able to exchange the 'respectable mummified humbug' of Kensington for 'life crude and impertinent perhaps, but living' seemed to her then and always the central significance of Bloomsbury. She felt herself for the first time fully alive, not only because of the lack of formality, but also because of the intellectual and artistic interests of the people she met there. Both Thoby and Adrian brought their Cambridge friends to the house more freely than they had at Hyde Park Gate. They also talked more freely about art and life, though completely frank discussion of sex came later. The presence of two attractive, unchaperoned sisters stimulated but also initially inhibited these debates, which had begun at Cambridge round about 1900 at meetings of the select group of Apostles and elsewhere. The young men were all disciples of G.E. Moore, who had written in his *Principia Ethica*: 'By far the most valuable things . . . are . . . the pleasures of human intercourse and the enjoyment of beautiful things; . . . it is they that form the rational ultimate end of social progress'. Moore's philosophy, with its emphasis on friendship, beauty and reason goes some way to explaining the Bloomsbury Group. Their belief in freedom of speech sprang from a determination to get at the truth, particularly about relationships and art. This could make them seem rather brutal at times, but it distinguished them, in Virginia's mind at least, from the polite

Kensington society she had left. Bloomsbury had 'bite', even if it hurt!

It was at Gordon Square in March 1905 that the first of the Bloomsbury Group's Thursday 'evenings' took place—with only two rather silent guests. Gradually these evenings became more lively, as the young men grew less shy of Thoby's sisters, and the talk became more interesting, though Virginia herself was more inclined to listen than to talk at this time. The guests varied but the nucleus remained the same—Lytton Strachey, Desmond MacCarthy, Saxon Sydney-Turner and Clive Bell. Leonard Woolf, who had been part of the group at Cambridge, met Virginia only briefly in 1904 before leaving for Ceylon, where he remained until 1911. Maynard Keynes, who had known the group at Cambridge, did not really become part of it until 1907, when he also introduced Duncan Grant. Roger Fry entered even later in 1910.

The need to give even a crude chronology of the Bloomsbury Group leads to a central problem in discussing it. For the members changed from time to time; those present at its Cambridge beginnings were not all *habitués* of 46 Gordon Square and when Virginia and Adrian left Gordon Square they were visited by other, younger people. The First World War also changed the nature of the group, so that Virginia was finally prompted to ask a friend in 1925, 'Who *is* Bloomsbury in your mind?' Like most people who discuss Bloomsbury she is herself contradictory, believing on the one hand that the headquarters of 'Bloomsbury' have always been in Gordon Square; on the other that 'Bloomsbury' was divided geographically into the various houses she occupied within the district itself. So that Lytton, Desmond and Saxon belong to the 'Cambridge stage of life [i.e. at Gordon Square]; very intellectual; cut free from Hyde Park Gate'; whereas Ka Cox, Rupert Brooke and Duncan Grant all

come later: 'they belong to the Fitzroy [Square] days'.
So she goes on, dividing them up both chronologically
and geographically. Yet one cannot help feeling that
what she refers to as 'Old Bloomsbury', which she
describes as 'six people with no special start, except
what their wits [gave] them', is for her the most significant phase in the group's development. The Thursday
'evenings' at Gordon Square were, she believes, the germ
from which sprang all that has since come to be called
Bloomsbury. For it was there that they 'worked out a
view of life which was not by any means corrupt or
sinister or merely intellectual; rather ascetic and austere
indeed . . .'

Who then were Virginia's six original members? Even
that is difficult to define, but it seems to come down to
Virginia and Vanessa, Lytton Strachey, Desmond
MacCarthy, Saxon Sydney-Turner and Clive Bell. These
last four certainly dominated the scene at 46 Gordon
Square. Though it was not the first time Virginia or
Vanessa had met their brothers' Cambridge friends, in
the new light of their independent existence they gained
fresh significance. Thoby had already made them seem
fascinating to Virginia as he described them on the long
country walks they took together, or sat over her fire in
her room.

'The Strache', or Lytton Strachey, was certainly the
most striking of these friends. He came from a large,
lively, upper-middle class family not dissimilar to the
Stephens, and brought various members of it into contact with the group. As a delicate child he had had a
rather erratic education, quite different from the more
formal public school variety of the other male members
of Bloomsbury and not unlike Virginia's own. This
probably accounted for his highly individualistic views,
which stood out even at Cambridge. He was regarded by
his contemporaries and tutors as decidedly eccentric,

both in appearance and behaviour. A tall, extremely thin figure with a droopy moustache (which later became a bushy red beard), he had a habit of lying coiled up like a snake in a chair, then suddenly attacking his victim with some devastating irony. This would be delivered in what came to be known as the 'Strachey voice', starting very low and ending up as a squeak. Thoby could imitate this voice to perfection, but he also took Lytton very seriously, describing him to Virginia as 'the essence of culture' with his French pictures and his passion for Pope. Not only was he a 'prodigy of wit', he was also thought to be academically brilliant: 'Whatever they give you, Strachey,' one tutor remarked, 'it won't be good enough'. Yet Lytton failed to get his predicted first and was turned down for a fellowship, perhaps because of his unconventional approach. His main interest by the time Virginia met him was writing, which naturally drew them together. Lytton was only at the experimental stage in the early 1900s, but he was to establish himself as a great innovator in his field of biography. The book which made him famous, *Eminent Victorians*, was a deliberate departure from the heavy Victorian 'Life and Letters' style. In this series of brief biographical sketches, Strachey set out to do the opposite, that is to *de*-mythify famous Victorian figures who had become legends in their own lifetime—Florence Nightingale, Gordon of Khartoum, Arnold of Rugby and Cardinal Manning. (Cardinal Newman escapes more lightly!) If his intention was to shock the public into an awareness of the truth behind the myths, he certainly succeeded, firmly establishing his reputation at the same time. Vanessa believed that his great honesty of mind and his hatred of sham was of great benefit to Bloomsbury, particularly in its early stages. Virginia, who could not deny the truth of this was, nevertheless more grudging. She was uncertain about the ultimate value of his writing. In her view it lacked originality. She linked this with what she regarded as the Strachey character—'prosaic, lacking magnanimity, shorn of atmosphere'. This failure of romance and vitality, she argued, produced 'that metallic and conventionally brilliant style' which prevented his writing from being first rate. Having accused Lytton of lacking originality, however, she found it hard to explain both his dominance of a whole generation at Cambridge and his radical innovations in biography. Since she undoubtedly felt threatened by his early success, she was forced to admit that it might be jealousy as a rival which prejudiced her view of his work. She also recalled his honesty, loyalty and 'great passion for the mind'. It was these qualities which caused her, in spite of his overt homosexuality, to accept his proposal of marriage in 1909. After it was hastily withdrawn she saw how undesirable it would have been: 'Had I married Lytton,' she wrote years later, 'I should never have written anything. . . . He checks and inhibits in the most curious way'. And yet of all the early Bloomsbury Group, he was the one she most enjoyed talking to, about books, feelings and life generally. After they were separated geographically by Lytton's move to the country they continued to discuss such matters in long, witty letters and at occasional meetings: 'We sit up talking,' Virginia wrote in 1927, 'about Queen Elizabeth, sodomy, love, the Antigone, Othello . . .'.

An equally brilliant but far less effectual member of the group was Desmond MacCarthy. The son of an Irish father and a German-French mother, Desmond seems to have inherited the Celt's charm and conversational gifts but nothing of the Teuton's practicality. (Leonard Woolf said that he was one of the most charming men he had ever met.) Desmond's father, a subagent of the Bank of England, thought it proper to have his only son educated at Eton and Cambridge, where Desmond duly went. In fact Desmond's background was altogether correct and when he came down from Cambridge, the year Thoby, Lytton, Clive Bell and Leonard Woolf arrived there, he went out into London society in the expected fashion. Here, incidentally, he caught glimpses of Virginia, Vanessa and their half-sister Stella, looking 'like a Greek slave'. Desmond also married 'well', a Molly Warre-Cornish, whose father was Vice-Provost of Eton. Though Molly was from a wealthy background, Desmond himself had very little money and was forced to find work. All his friends, who thought him enormously talented, predicted that he would write a 'great work', but in the meantime he took up criticism, an agreeable profession he decided, as long as he could get enough work. Later on he became editor of the *New Statesman*, to which he contributed a weekly column under the pseudonym 'Affable Hawk'. He also produced a number of volumes of mainly dramatic criticism. Meanwhile the 'great work' never materialized except, as Virginia put it, 'in that hour between tea and dinner, when so many things appear not merely possible but achieved'. Both she and other friends tried to organize Desmond into writing the fabled book, even at one point arranging to have a secretary hidden in the room at dinner to take down the brilliant conversation which made people believe in Desmond's genius. Still nothing materialized. Was it 'slackness of fibre,' Virginia wondered, that prevented Desmond achieving things, or was it the more attractive and imaginative sense that 'things don't altogether matter'? Whatever it was, it made Desmond an infuriating but lovable friend over many years. 'I'm not sure,' Virginia wrote in 1919 'that he hasn't the nicest nature of any of us'. Just as she felt overwhelmed by his vagueness and apparent lack of awareness, he would once again charm her by his sensitivity and intelligence. He may be, as his wife confided to Virginia 'a little spoilt, terribly without a will, and much at the mercy of any fine lady or gentleman with good wine', but his conversation remained as brilliant as ever and his sympathy as all-embracing.

Desmond's loquaciousness was more than balanced in the group by Saxon Sydney-Turner's silence. Though Thoby told Virginia that Saxon's talk was also of astonishing brilliance, to begin with she heard scarcely a word from him. By 'brilliance', however, Thoby meant not 'wit', but 'truth': Saxon was the most brilliant talker he knew because he always spoke the truth. Thoby's 'prodigy of learning' had been born at Hove, the son of a doctor who kept mentally deficient patients in his house. A scholar at Westminster, he also gained a scholarship to Trinity, where he shared rooms with Leonard Woolf and got to know Lytton, Thoby and Clive. A short, thin man with a pale face and straw-coloured hair, Saxon's physical insignificance was compensated for by a reputation for wisdom and great erudition, particularly in maths and music. Thoby terrified Virginia by telling her that Saxon had the whole of Greek literature by heart and that there was practically nothing in any language worthwhile that he had not read. At Cambridge he never came out by day, but might tap on one's window late at night like a moth and then, at about 3 in the morning, begin to talk. It was partly the nature of this talk, with its curious hesitations and convolutions that made Leonard see him as a character from an unwritten novel by Henry James. When Saxon left Cambridge he became a civil servant in the Treasury, where he seemed to Leonard gradually to withdraw from life, 'to protect himself from its impact and from the impact of persons, emotions and things by spinning round himself an elaborate and ingenious series of cocoons'. Though he continued to write poems, paint pictures and compose sonatas, like Desmond Saxon never achieved the 'great book' that had been predicted. Virginia was clearly as fond of him as she was of Desmond and found him equally maddening. It has been suggested

that she considered the possibility of marrying Saxon
early on. It is difficult to imagine her being able to see
him in this role, however, since Saxon seems to have
shared neither Lytton's homosexual, nor Desmond's
and Clive's heterosexual interests. He told Virginia he
was a sadist and Leonard believed him to be a eunuch.
Virginia preferred to see him more fancifully as a
'phantom, gliding like a moonbeam' through Bloomsbury's early gatherings. Later on she compared him,
only half-teasingly, to the aloe that flowers once in a
hundred years, snow falling by moonlight, frozen water
and a closed bud. Yet she truly admired his gentleness
and found his lack of virility compensated for by his
wisdom, goodness and sensitivity.

Clive Bell suffered from none of Saxon's reticence. At
first sight he is the most extrovert of the group. Brought
up in the country, where he grew to love outdoor activities at an early age, he seemed to Leonard Woolf, when
he first saw him at Trinity, a typically hearty, non-
intellectual product of a wealthy background and good,
middle-range, public school (Marlborough):

> The first time I ever saw him he was walking through
> Great Court in full hunting rig-out, including — unless
> this is wishful imagination — a hunting-horn and the
> whip carried by the whipper-in. He was a great horse-
> man and a first-rate shot, very well-off, and to be seen
> in the company of 'bloods', not the rowing, cricket
> and rugby blues, but the rich young men who shot,
> and hunted, and rode in the point-to-point races. He
> had a very attractive face, particularly to women, boy-
> ish, good-humoured, hair red and curly, and what in
> the eighteenth century was called, I think, a sanguine
> complexion.

There was obviously more to Clive than this description

suggests. For one thing his background was not as solid as Leonard first imagined. The Bells were relative new-comers to the complicated English class system, not solidly upper-middle class like the Stephens or the Stracheys. They had only recently made enough money in coal to move into their sham Tudor mansion in Wilt-shire. Clive himself seemed at times ashamed of his family and the first thing he did on arriving at Cambridge was to rebel against its philistinism. Thoby, Clive's closest friend there, told Virginia that Bell had never opened a book till he came to Trinity in 1899, when he suddenly discovered Shelley and Keats and went nearly mad with excitement. 'He's a sort of mixture between Shelley and a sporting country squire,' Thoby concluded, giving Virginia a fantastic impression of a kind of sun-god—with straw in his hair. From having been almost entirely non-intellectual Clive became obsessed not only with poetry and philosophy, but also with modern art, which remained his life-long interest. Not an 'original' like Virginia or Lytton, he nevertheless produced a number of serious books of art criticism and a large philosophical book on *Civilization*. Yet his friends never seem to have taken him quite seriously as an intellectual, perhaps finding it impossible to reconcile this with his pronounced hedonistic streak. Leonard, who painted an unflattering portrait of him in his novel *The Wise Virgins*, placed Clive some distance from the centre of the inner circle of intellectuals and scholars formed at Trinity round G.E. Moore. Nor was Clive ever invited to join the Apostles, that élite Cambridge secret society to which anyone of outstanding intellect was normally elected. Lytton, whilst acknowledging the complexity of Clive's personality, maintained that there was a layer of stupidity which ran transversely through all the other layers. Even Virginia, who was very fond of Clive and had a prolonged flirtation with him in 1908, reflects

the ambivalence most of Clive's friends felt towards him.
On the one hand she admired his genuine interest in
philosophy and art; on the other she rather despised his
dilettantism, which manifested itself in his flamboyant
clothes, expensive tastes and innumerable affairs with
worldly ladies. She and Vanessa privately named him
'the parakeet'. In short Clive was a mass of contradictions,
which intrigued the novelist in Virginia. 'Clive is a great
source of pleasure to me,' she wrote nearly twenty years
after meeting him, 'for one thing because he says out-
right what I spend my life in concealing. Never was there
anyone so petty, conceited, open and good at bottom of
heart. I always think of him as a mixture of Pepys and
Boswell'. Whereas with Lytton Virginia talked mainly
about books, with Clive she talked about love. Indeed it
was Clive who first introduced that dubious subject into
46 Gordon Square, by falling in love almost immediately
with Vanessa. When he declared himself in the summer
of 1905, Thoby shared Virginia's grim reaction to the
idea of their sister being taken away from them. On this
first occasion Vanessa turned Clive down, though not
without giving him some hope. Just over a year later she
accepted him, under rather desperate circumstances.

In November 1906 Virginia's elder brother, Thoby,
died. His death was particularly shocking in its sudden-
ness. Returning from a family holiday to Greece with a
high temperature, Thoby had been treated incorrectly
for malaria. Less than three weeks later he was dead —
of typhoid. His death was the second in under two years,
the fourth in only ten years for Virginia. As she paced
round Gordon Square, trying to understand why *she*
should have to suffer so much, she saw herself between
two great grindstones, which she must fight. Surprisingly
she did not have a nervous breakdown as she had after
her mother's, father's and Stella's deaths. She had
perhaps learnt to deal with disaster, for there is no doubt

that she felt very strongly indeed about Thoby. This
emerges not only in her letters and diaries of subsequent
years, but also in two of her most interesting novels,
Jacob's Room and *The Waves*. In both books she
attempts to capture Thoby's essence, just as she tried to
portray her father and mother in *To the Lighthouse*.
Jacob's Room follows Jacob, in a series of brief scenes,
from his childhood to his early and unexpected death. It
shows his stubbornness as a child refusing to give up a
skull he has found on the beach in Cornwall, his
romanticism in choosing Byron as a parting present from
his tutor, his passion for butterflies, his rebellion against
the dreariness of academic lunches at Cambridge, his love
of poetry, his attractiveness to women, his sensitivity
and his kindness. Throughout the novel the narrator
stresses the impossibility of trying to 'sum people up'.
The only phrase she will allow to stand for Jacob, which
obviously applied to Thoby, is 'so distinguished-looking'.
In *The Waves* even this shred of certainty has disappeared
and the reader is left to deduce from the six main
characters' reflections on Percy, alias Thoby, that he
represents a more than life-size 'norm', a middle way
between the intellectuals and the sportsmen. Their
impression of Percy as a rather heavy, clumsy little school-
boy with a straight nose and striking blue eyes, whose
determination and strong sense of justice manifests itself in terrifying rages, reflects Virginia's own memories
of Thoby as a child. 'Napoleonic' was one of the words
used of him. He was not so much 'clever' as gifted,
particularly at drawing. His Latin and Greek were rough,
the masters said, but his essays showed great intelligence.
Virginia remembered how, on first coming back from
prep. school, he told her all about the Greeks, whilst
walking up and down stairs to cover his embarrassment.
He continued to share his interests with her when he
went on to Clifton, having failed to win a scholarship to

Eton. Thoby also helped Virginia to run the family
magazine, *The Hyde Park Gate News*, initially. To some
extent Virginia had forced her way in between Thoby
and Vanessa, who were very close, and abandoned Adrian,
who felt it very keenly. The closeness of the three older
Stephen children was partly a result of their mother's
and Stella's death. This was cemented by their father's
death in 1904, when Thoby naturally became the head
of the family. Life at 46 Gordon Square was built up to
a large extent round him and his Cambridge friends. One
of the closest of these, Leonard Woolf, gives a memorable picture of 'the Goth', as Thoby was nicknamed:

> He gave one an impression of physical magnificence.
> He was six foot two, broad-shouldered and somewhat
> heavily made, with a small head set elegantly upon
> the broad shoulders so that it reminded one of the way
> in which the small head is set upon the neck of a well-
> bred Arab horse. His face was extraordinarily beautiful
> and his character was as beautiful as his face. In his
> monolithic character, his monolithic common-sense,
> his monumental judgements he continually reminded
> one of Dr Johnson, but a Samuel Johnson who had
> shed his neuroticism, his irritability, his fears. He had
> a perfect 'natural' style of writing . . . And there was
> a streak of the same natural style in his talk. Any wild
> statement, speculative judgement or Strachean
> exaggeration would be met with a 'Nonsense, my
> good fellow', from Thoby, and then a sentence of
> profound, but humorous common-sense, and a delight-
> ed chuckle. Thoby had a good sense of humour, a
> fine, sound, but not brilliant mind. . . . But what
> everyone who knew him remembers most vividly in
> him was his extraordinary charm. He had greater
> personal charm than anyone I have ever known, and,
> unlike other great 'charmers', he seemed, and I

believe was, entirely unconscious of it.

Leonard places Thoby near the centre of the circle of
scholars and intellectuals at Cambridge. Thoby was not
elected to the Apostles, however, which suggests that he
was not thought to be as intellectually brilliant as his
friends, with the exception of Clive Bell. Like Clive, too,
he was fond of physical activities. When he came down
from Cambridge in 1904 he took up law rather than
join Lytton and Desmond in their attempts to become
writers. Virginia saw him as a successful judge, just as
Mrs Ramsay imagines her son James 'all red and ermine
on the bench'. Reading between the lines it is clear that
both family and friends found Thoby a wholly depend-
able, very lovable, but not highly exciting. In the early
Bloomsbury Group this made him something of an
exception. His very lack of intellectual brilliance
probably made him easier to talk to and Virginia was
still very dependent on him in 1906. His death left her
feeling not only deprived, but even more vulnerable. At
twenty-four she had no serious prospect of marriage, no
real success as a writer and no close friend apart from
Vanessa. However, Vanessa, in her shock, had agreed to
marry Clive and they were to take over Gordon Square.
This left Virginia with Adrian to look for another house.

Vanessa's marriage early in 1907 marked the end of
the first chapter of Bloomsbury, according to Virginia:
'It had been very austere, very exciting, of immense
importance. . . . Now that Clive had shocked the Maxses,
the Booths, the Cecils, the Protheroes [i.e. all Stephen
family friends] irretrievably, now that the house was
done up once more, now that they were giving little
parties with their beautiful brown table linen and their
lovely eighteenth-century silver, Bloomsbury rapidly
lost the monastic character it had had in Chapter One;
the character of Chapter Two was superficially at least

to be very different'. For one thing, there was a much
freer, perhaps even obsessional discussion of sex, such
as the memorable occasion when Lytton, seeing a stain
on Vanessa's white dress, asked dramatically, 'semen?'

29 Fitzroy Square (1907-1911)

The most obvious change for Virginia, however, was
geographical. She had grown increasingly fond of Gordon
Square in the two years she had lived there and was not
at all happy to leave. Wherever she and Adrian moved it
must be within walking distance, though tact demanded
that it should not be too near the newly-weds. So when
they discovered a house only a short walk away across
Tottenham Court Road, they decided to take it. Number
29, in the south-west corner of the spacious Fitzroy
Square, had been lived in by Bernard Shaw and his
mother in the 1890s. It was in some ways similar to 46
Gordon Square, with its basement, rendered façade,
balcony and decorative railings. But, as Virginia herself
recognised, both the house, with its elegantly curved
ground floor windows, and the square with its fine
Adam façades, classical pillars, frieze and great urn in
the middle, had more distinction than Gordon Square.
On the other hand it was decidedly more derelict by
the time Virginia and Adrian moved there. The houses
of the rich had gradually decayed and been taken over
as offices, lodgings, nursing homes and small artisans'
workshops. Duncan Grant, who had taken two rooms
on the second floor of number 22, on the same side of
the square, wrote:

There was certainly not much gentility left in the
district; the only relic of grandeur was a beadle to
march round the square to keep order among the

children, in a top-hat and a tail-coat piped with red and brass buttons. The Stephens were the only people I remember who had a complete house there; complete with their cook Sophy Farrell, their maid Maud, a front-door bell and a dog, Hans.

Maynard Keynes joined Duncan later at number 22 and in 1913 Roger Fry started his Omega Workshop at number 33, where it remained until its closure in 1919. Vanessa rented a studio round the corner at 8 Fitzroy Street in 1929.

In 1907, however, Virginia and Adrian were on their own in the square, apart from Duncan who developed a close friendship with Adrian. Though there was one floor less than at Gordon Square, there were half the number of inhabitants, so the two younger Stephens spread themselves accordingly. On the ground floor were the dining-room and Adrian's book-lined study, on the second floor Virginia's rooms, full of books and papers, and above that Adrian's bedroom. The whole of the first floor was made into a drawing-room, with double doors and long windows looking out on to the square. Virginia, who was more old-fashioned, or less avant-garde, than her sister, furnished this room with red brocade Chinese curtains, a green carpet and an old-fashioned pianola, which Adrian played by the hour. She also hung a Watts portrait of her father in pride of place. In the basement, as usual, reigned Sophy Farrell, who had moved first with the Stephen children to Gordon Square, then with Virginia and Adrian to Fitzroy Square. She had not found it easy to decide which household to stay with, but felt that Virginia needed her more: 'She's such a harum scarum thing she wouldn't know if they sold her. She don't know what she has on her plate'. Besides Sophy there was also the maid, Maud, and looking back Virginia felt that they had lived in comparative

3. *29 Fitzroy Square*, off Tottenham Court Road: the house
Virginia shared with Adrian
after Vanessa's marriage in
1907.

splendour – 'a maid, carpets, fires'.

There were some drawbacks to the new house. Family friends and relatives made the usual protests about the seediness of the neighbourhood, which were, as usual, ignored. More seriously for Virginia Fitzroy Square was also very noisy, sandwiched as it was between Tottenham Court Road, Euston Road and Great Portland Street. 'Fitzroy Square,' she wrote later, 'rubbed a nerve bare which will never sleep again while an omnibus is in the neighbourhood'. She had double-glazing installed in her study, but still found it difficult to concentrate on her work. And, having just given up teaching at Morley College, her writing was more important to her than ever.

By far the greatest drawback for Virginia at Fitzroy Square, however, was having to share it with Adrian. As far as she was concerned, they were the most incompatible of people. They had frequent rows, which usually ended with them throwing pats of butter at each other. Without Vanessa and Thoby's restraining influence, the younger Stephens real differences emerged. Yet it is almost certain that these differences were based on Virginia's and Adrian's basic similarities. Both had been far more nervous and sensitive as children than their elder brother and sister. Whereas Virginia remembered Thoby as a solid, aggressive little boy, she thought of Adrian as 'appealing, childish' and something of a mother's boy: 'Him she cherished separately; she called him "My Joy".' Virginia believed that Adrian, like herself, was a typical Stephen. He was undoubtedly as neurotic as she was. Like her, too, he grew to be tall and thin. Henry James, an old friend of the Stephen family, seeing Adrian and Virginia together at Rye during the summer of 1907 described the former as 'interminably long and dumb', marching beside Virginia 'like a giraffe beside an ostrich – save that Virginia is facially most fair'. As a child, however, Adrian had been stunted

enough to be called 'dwarf' and 'blue mouse'. He had
also been thought too vulnerable to send away to school
like Thoby, but had been a day boy, first at Evelyns, then
Westminster. By the time he reached Cambridge Thoby
and his friends were already beginning to come down.
Once again Adrian must have felt excluded, for there is
little doubt that he saw himself as an outsider, both with
his siblings and with their friends. When psychoanalysed
at the age of forty, he blamed his 'tragedy', as he called
it, on his brother and sisters, particularly Virginia. Instead
of pairing off with her younger brother, she had tagged
along after Thoby and Vanessa, leaving Adrian very
much on his own. Adrian's reaction had been rather
obvious. He had refused to join in, with such family
activities as butterfly-hunting, and had set up two rival
journals to Virginia and Thoby's *Hyde Park Gate News*.
At Cambridge he had reacted against the fashionable
worship of Moore, but had not been intellectually
brilliant enough to carry such rebellions off and ended
up seeming rather pathetic. Adrian had undertaken
psychoanalysis in these pioneer days in order to prepare
himself for a career in psychiatry. Though called to the
bar, he had never practised and eventually turned to
medicine, partly in response to his own problems. Unlike
Virginia he had *not* broken down in response to the
numerous family deaths, but he clearly regarded himself as a damaged person. Apart from a few scattered
references — to his 'utter lackadaisicalness', for example —
Virginia says noticeably little about him in her memoirs,
letters and diaries. Her most positive remark is rather
vague and lukewarm: 'I think it absurd to call Adrian a
bore; he has great distinction; not that I could ever live
with him tolerably'. Nor has Adrian attracted much
attention from subsequent writers on Bloomsbury. The
picture which emerges is even less clear than that of
Thoby. It is the Stephen sisters who have left their mark.

Virginia attributed much of her unhappiness and sense of failure at Fitzroy Square to living with Adrian. Initially they had been united by Thoby's death and the excitement of setting up house together, but the situation quickly deteriorated. Adrian, who was as sardonic as his father, teased Virginia almost continually, perhaps in an attempt to deal with her vagueness and volatility. Certainly they drove each other into frenzies of irritation and the depths of gloom. Even their Thursday evenings, which they had set up in competition with 46 Gordon Square, seemed to Virginia a failure.

Yet Virginia's enforced independence from Vanessa and, of course, Thoby, must have given her greater confidence. She had become mistress of her own home, however nervously she managed it. She also began to rent her own country house, Little Talland (see pages 224-227), during this period. She was writing more successfully. In addition to occasional pieces for *The Times Literary Supplement*, she had begun reviewing regularly for *The Weekly Guardian*. Most significantly of all, she had at last started work on a novel, *Melymbrosia*, which eventually became *The Voyage Out*. She and Adrian had even started a second 'evening' on Fridays, when they held poetry and play readings. Furthermore their Thursday evenings which Virginia described so gloomily created a second centre for Bloomsbury, though for Virginia there was only ever one centre—Gordon Square. Partly because of its geographical position, Fitzroy Square attracted a number of interesting new members. Duncan Grant, who lived only a few doors away at number 22, was one of the most intriguing of these.

Duncan, who was three years younger than Virginia, first met her and Adrian in Paris, where they had joined Vanessa and Clive on their honeymoon in 1907. Duncan was in Paris to study painting. The only child of an Army officer, he had spent a restless childhood travelling between India and England until he settled down with his cousin, Lytton Strachey's family. After a conventional and not academically brilliant career at Hillbrow and St Paul's, his aunt, Lady Strachey, had persuaded his parents to let him study painting at Westminster School of Art. He made no particular mark there and was turned down by the Royal Academy School. By the time Virginia met him he had studied in Italy and spent a year under Jacques-Emile Blanche in Paris. He was still unknown but undeterred. Perhaps as a result of his meeting with the younger Stephens, Duncan took a studio in Fitzroy Square a few months later. He was a frequent visitor at number 29 and Virginia heard many lurid stories about his fellowlodgers, a drunken old charwoman and a crazed clergyman. Duncan got on well with both these characters, but then his attitude to life seemed entirely relaxed, apart from his determination to become a painter. His lack of money did not worry him; there were always friends to give him cast-off clothing, meals and other more exotic things. Virginia, for example, lent him her father's dress trousers and some old china to paint. Typically, he broke the china and ruined the trousers by jumping into a canal to rescue a drowning child. Virginia's first impression of him — 'a queer, faun-like figure, hitching his clothes up, blinking his eyes, stumbling oddly over the long words in his sentences' — captures the sense of vagueness he conveyed to the outside world. In time she came to see that vagueness as deceptive. Duncan may have appeared to be vaguely tossing about in the breeze but he always alighted exactly where he meant to. Beneath a strikingly charming exterior, which led D.H. Lawrence to call him 'a dark-skinned taciturn Hamlet', Duncan concealed a well-defined character. Virginia called him 'old convolvulus bed' because the image conveyed his 'voluptuous creamy grace' but also his 'deadly' tenacity. His undoubted hedonism was completely free of laziness. One of the least ambitious members of Bloomsbury, he was yet motivated to work extremely hard at his painting and, if necessary, at housework too. When he and Vanessa, after various other relationships, set up house together and produced a daughter, Duncan showed himself capable of great unselfishness and discipline in running it. His outstanding quality, according to Virginia, was sympathy. His complete openness to life enabled him to respond fully to people. He enjoyed both homosexual and hetero-sexual relationships in a way which reminds one of Virginia herself and there is the same sensual quality in both their works. Unlike Virginia, however, his intense response to both people and objects was combined with a down-to-earthness which Virginia called 'sanity'. This accounted for his solidity, in contrast with her own instability.

Duncan's entry to Bloomsbury reinforced the visual side of the group previously represented by Vanessa and Clive alone. It seems appropriate that he should have replaced Clive in Vanessa's affections later. In 1907, however, Duncan was deeply involved with Maynard Keynes who, like himself, was sexually versatile. (Maynard later made a satisfactory marriage to the Russian ballerina, Lydia Lopokova, whilst Duncan fathered Vanessa's third child.) Duncan reintroduced Maynard to Bloomsbury, in a sense. For Maynard had met some of the members briefly at Cambridge. Having gone up to King's College in 1902, however, he had missed most of them, since only Leonard and Adrian had remained for a fourth year. By the time Maynard started visiting Virginia and Adrian in Fitzroy Square, Leonard was in Ceylon. So that Maynard was virtually a new member. He established himself so firmly, however, that when Virginia tried to analyse 'Bloomsbury' ten years later, she described him as 'the chief fount of the

magic spirit'. In many ways Maynard epitomises all that
was socially and intellectually acceptable to the group,
who were largely unaware of their own snobbishness.
The son of a Cambridge don and a politically active
mother, Maynard added the further advantage of scholarships to both Eton and King's. At Cambridge he quickly
became a disciple of Moore and was elected to the
Apostles in his first year, an almost unheard of privilege.
By 1909, when he was sharing Duncan's rooms in
Fitzroy Square, he had become a Fellow of King's. His
radical theories in economics impressed the British Government so much that he was asked to join the Treasury
during the First World War. This he did, to the disgust
of his mainly pacifist friends. He also represented the
British Government at the Peace Conference in 1919.
His disagreement with the other members of the
delegation and his resignation led him to write *The
Economic Consequences of the Peace*, which made him
world famous. In fact Maynard was the most outwardly
successful of the Bloomsbury Group and for many
people is the greatest figure to emerge from it. Of all the
inhabitants of 46 Gordon Square, it is Maynard who
has been chosen for the blue commemmorative plaque.
Though physically unprepossessing—he was sometimes
compared to a gorilla, with his thick lips and slight
shamble—Maynard made a very positive impression on
those who met him. Virginia's first impression of him
was 'very truculent, very formidable, like a portrait of
Tolstoy as a young man'. His wit reminded her of quick-
silver on a sloping board. Under his daunting intellect,
however, she detected 'a kind and even simple heart'.
She also admired his lack of snobbishness, though a more
cynical observer might see this as a result of his own
social privilege and confidence.

Another, more erratic member to join Bloomsbury in
the Fitzroy Square days was E.M. Forster—'Morgan' to

his friends. Like Maynard he was not an exact con-
temporary of the early male members of the group. Two
years older than most of them, he only met them briefly
during his last, and their first year at Cambridge. Leonard
seems to have been closest to him; certainly he remembered Morgan during his King's College days. He found him
a 'strange, elusive, evasive' person who, in the middle
of the most intimate conversation, would suddenly withdraw into himself. Leonard detected the same subtlety,
sensibility and odd humour in the man as in the novels
and short stories he had already started to write.
(Morgan was to publish *Pharos and Pharillon* with
Leonard later at the Hogarth Press.) Lytton nicknamed
Morgan the Taupe, partly because of his slight physical
resemblance to a mole, but chiefly because he seemed
'intellectually and emotionally to travel unseen underground and every now and again pop up unexpectedly
with some subtle observation or delicate quip which
somehow or other he had found in the depths of the
earth or of his own soul'. Virginia preferred to see him
as a blue butterfly. This she felt conveyed his transparency
and lightness, for Morgan was always flitting from place
to place. After Cambridge, which he describes in *The
Longest Journey*, he went to Italy, the main setting for
A Room with a View, then on to India, the mystic background to *A Passage to India* and finally Egypt. His only
fixed point was his old mother, with whom he shared a
house in Surrey — 'like mice in a nest', as Virginia fancifully put it. Perhaps because of his homosexuality, which
he never openly acknowledged, he formed no other lasting relationship in those early days, though he had many
friends. Virginia liked him greatly, whilst finding him
'whimsical and vagulous' to an extent that frightened her
with her own 'clumsiness and definiteness'. Despite his
vagueness she knew him to have a very clear idea of what
he believed, particularly when it came to writing. Morgan,

who had embarked on his fiction long before Virginia,
influenced her own early work, but they never really
agreed on the role of fiction. Virginia found him rather
prosaically concerned with 'message'—too near the fact,
as she might have put it—whilst he found her
dangerously ready to abandon content for technique.
They remained good friends, however, and Virginia
continued to value his criticism, mainly because she
thought it completely objective.

Apart from E.M. Forster, there were other occasional
visitors to Fitzroy Square who remained, like him, on
the fringes of Bloomsbury. The most famous of these
was Rupert Brooke, whose relationship with Virginia
has been much publicised. Having met briefly in Cornwall as children, they renewed their acquaintance on
one of Virginia's visits to Cambridge, probably through
Lytton or Maynard, who were mutual friends. Virginia
spent a week with Rupert at Grantchester, when she
found him 'all that could be called kind and interesting
and substantial and goodhearted'. She was not impressed
by his poetry, which he read aloud to her on the lawn,
but she did admire 'his gift with people', his 'sanity'
and 'force'. Adrian referred to her 'Rupert Romance'
but it is most unlikely that this existed. She boasted of
her nude midnight bathes with him, but she was as close
to his regular girl-friend, Katharine ('Ka') Cox, as she
was to him. She also got to know other of Rupert's
friends, the 'Neo-Pagans' as they came to be called, and
entertained them occasionally at Fitzroy Square. Ka
Cox, Gwen Darwin and Jacques Raverat remained life-
long friends, but none of them could be said to be true
members of Bloomsbury. In fact Bloomsbury was rather
against Rupert and he against them, though Virginia
kept her private version of him, which she stuck to when
they all cried him down.

Here, like Virginia, it becomes necessary to ask—where

does Bloomsbury end? Does it, for instance, include
Bedford Square, the home of Lady Ottoline Morrell,
daughter of General Arthur Bentinck and Lady Bolsover?
Virginia was convinced that Ottoline deserved at least
one chapter in the history of Bloomsbury, and that that
chapter began during the Fitzroy days. One Thursday
evening 'the Ott.' had swooped down on Virginia and
Adrian, with her husband Philip and Augustus John and
his wife. The next morning she wrote to demand the
names and addresses of all Virginia's 'wonderful friends'
and followed this up with an open invitation to her own
Thursday 'evenings' at Bedford Square. Virginia went with
Rupert Brooke and quickly found herself swept into 'that
extraordinary whirlpool where such odd sticks and straws
were brought momentarily together':

> There was Augustus John, very sinister in a black
> stock and a velvet coat: Winston Churchill, very
> rubicund, all gold lace and medals, on his way to
> Buckingham Palace; Raymond Asquith crackling with
> epigrams; Francis Dodd telling me most graphically
> how he and Aunt Susie had killed bugs: . . . There
> was Lord Henry Bentinck at one end of the sofa and
> perhaps Nina Lamb at the other. There was Philip
> [Morrell] fresh from the House of Commons hum-
> ming and hawing on the hearthrug. There was Gilbert
> Cannan who was said to be in love with Ottoline.
> There was Bertie Russell, whom she was said to be in
> love with. Above all, there was Ottoline herself.

Virginia's first impression of Ottoline was of a great
lady who, discontented with her own class, had turned
to artists and writers for satisfaction. Her great gift was
to make life seem amusing, interesting and adventurous.
Ottoline appeared to Virginia then like a Spanish galleon
hung with golden coins and silken sails. Later Virginia

felt that the sails had become rat-eaten and the masts
mouldy, but the grandeur remained. And Virginia herself continued to be fascinated, if exasperated, by
Ottoline's strange mixture of humbleness, splendour
and hypocrisy.

Altogether Virginia led a very active social life at
Fitzroy Square. It was a rather adventurous one for a
woman of her class and time. Bloomsbury had become
sexually liberated, yet she herself remained frightened
of sex. 'My terror of real life,' she wrote of her Fitzroy
days, 'has always kept me in a nunnery. And much
of this talking and adventuring in London alone, and
sitting up to all hours with young men, and saying
what came first, was rather petty; . . . at least narrow;
circumscribed; and leading to endless ramifications of
intrigue. We had violent rows—oh yes, I used to rush
through London in such rages, and stormed Hampstead
heights at night in white or purple fury'. Consciously or
not, Virginia was looking for a husband. Her increasing
sexual awareness made her predominantly homosexual
friends seem rather boring. Whilst still appreciating the
honesty and simplicity of relationships with homosexuals,
she had begun to want more from male company.
Desmond and Clive were already married, Maynard and
Duncan bi-sexuals and Leonard Woolf was in Ceylon.
There was an unsatisfactory relationship with Walter
Lamb, the painter, who later contributed to the portrait
of 'the admirable Hugh Whitbread' in *Mrs Dalloway*, and
two other friends, Sydney Waterlow and Walter Headlam,
showed some interest in her. The only possible suitor at
Fitzroy Square, however, seemed to be Hilton Young, a
childhood friend who renewed his acquaintance with the
Stephens in Bloomsbury. He was very much attracted to
Virginia but when he did eventually propose she said she
did not love him enough to accept. Indeed the only
person she could consider seriously was Lytton, whom

she was willing to marry in spite of his homosexuality.
Yet Lytton himself, having proposed, wisely realised the
impossibility of such a marriage and recanted. In her
desperation, and possibly out of jealousy towards her
sister's apparently secure marriage, Virginia entered into
a prolonged flirtation with Clive, which hurt Vanessa
deeply. It was no wonder Virginia remembered herself
as 'devilish unhappy' and 'at war with the whole world'
in Fitzroy Square.

38 Brunswick Square (1911-1912)

In October 1911 the lease of 29 Fitzroy Square expired.
Virginia and Adrian had already decided to look for a
large house to share with friends, who might help to ease
the friction between them. After looking at another,
bigger house in Fitzroy Square and one near Ottoline
Morrell in Bedford Square, they finally settled on 38
Brunswick Square. They were still approximately the
same distance from Gordon Square, that is, close enough
to walk but not too close for comfort. Brunswick Square
was, however, more authentically 'Bloomsbury' and not
nearly as noisy as Fitzroy Square. It was also nearer to
the City, which Virginia loved, particularly for walking.
Most of the square, including number 38, has since been
demolished; the north side was pulled down about 1936
and replaced by the School of Pharmacy, and the west
side, badly damaged in the Second World War, was then
cleared in the 1970s to make way for the Bloomsbury
Shopping Centre. None of the south side survives and the
east side continues to adjoin Mecklenburgh Square and
Coram's Fields.

Virginia looked out on Brunswick Square from the
north side, where number 38 was situated next to the
Foundling Hospital at number 40, now rechristened The

Coram Trust'. This Foundling Hospital became something of a joke among the younger Stephens, since Vanessa used it to allay George Duckworth's fears about Virginia sharing a house alone with four young men, even if one of them was her brother! Violet Dickinson, whom Virginia still adored, was brought in to try to dissuade her, but in vain. Virginia was perfectly happy to share the house with Duncan Grant, Maynard Keynes, Adrian and Leonard Woolf.

Duncan and Maynard occupied the ground floor, where Duncan decorated the curving wall of their drawing room with a lively London street scene, in what Vanessa called his 'leopard' style. Duncan also helped paint a mural for Adrian's rooms on the first floor — a tennis game in the style of Matisse. Adrian, with an amateur's enthusiasm, added several nudes to various cupboard doors. The most prominent feature of Virginia's rooms on the second floor was books and papers, usually in a state of some disorder. Above her, in what would originally have been the servants' smaller, less elegant rooms, was Leonard Woolf, who had been invited to join the 'commune' on his return for long leave from Ceylon. Presumably those at the top paid less than those at the bottom of the house and it is interesting to note that Virginia and Leonard, both very economically minded, should occupy the two top floors.

As at Fitzroy Square Sophy Farrell reigned in the basement, together with the housemaid, Maud. Meals were to be provided on request and rules were drawn up to cover this. Breakfast was at 9 a.m., lunch at 1 p.m.. tea at 4.30 p.m. and dinner at 8 p.m. Trays were to be placed in the hall punctually at the appropriate time. 'Inmates' were requested to carry up their own trays and to carry down their dirty dishes as soon as they had finished their meal. They were also requested to put their initials on the 'Kitchen Instruction Tablet' in the

4. *38 Brunswick Square, Blooms-bury*: the house Virginia and Adrian shared with Maynard Keynes, Duncan Grant and Leonard Woolf after the lease of Fitzroy Square expired in 1911.

hall against all meals required that day.

When the inhabitants of 'Brunswick' tired of the tray system, they would go round to Gordon Square, where the larder always held enough for a few unexpected guests. Gordon Square in turn visited 'Brunswick', where they were well entertained by Maynard's champagne — often in his absence. On summer evenings they would all sit in the garden, which was, literally, 'deathly' quiet, backing as it did on to a graveyard. According to Vanessa, 'all sorts of parties at all hours of the day or night happened constantly'. Brunswick Square, though briefer than the previous two, marked a very sociable phase in the history of Bloomsbury.

Virginia tended to divide her friends according to where she first got to know them. Brunswick Square made her think of 'the Oliviers and all that set', but the four daughters of the Fabian Socialist, Sir Sydney Olivier, never became close friends and were certainly never central to Bloomsbury. Far more importantly, both for the group and for Virginia herself were Roger Fry and Leonard Woolf. Though both Roger and Leonard had visited the Stephens at Fitzroy Square, it was at Brunswick Square that Virginia got to know them properly.

Roger Fry was introduced to Bloomsbury by Clive Bell, who thought him the most interesting person he had met since his Cambridge days. (It was in a train returning from Cambridge with Vanessa that Clive first met him.) Virginia recalled Roger's appearance among them 'in a large ulster coat, every pocket of which was stuffed with a book, a paint box or something intriguing; . . . he had canvases [*sic*] under his arms; his hair flew; his eyes glowed'. More than ten years older than most of them, Roger struck them all as having far more knowledge and experience of life. He had left Cambridge long before Thoby, Clive, Leonard and the others arrived and had, of course, been an Apostle. Curiously, he had read

Science, though quickly rejected it in favour of painting. This had greatly upset his highly puritanical Quaker family, particularly his father, who had made a name for himself in Law. Leonard felt that in spite of his apparent rebellion, Roger remained a Quaker at heart. He had the Quaker's uncompromising sense of public duty and responsibility, together with the Quaker's ethical austerity. This may help to explain a certain ruthlessness in Roger which led, on the one hand, to him dumping unwanted visitors on his friends, and on the other, to him being a brilliant art dealer. Not only could he recognise the worth of a picture, however obscure its painter, but he could also drive a hard bargain in buying it. For this reason he had been asked by the Metropolitan Museum of New York to help them form their famous art collection.

By the time Roger arrived in Bloomsbury in 1910 he had separated from the Metropolitan Museum. His personal life had also reached a crisis, with the realization that his wife was incurably insane. Bloomsbury was to fill both gaps, firstly by encouraging and helping him with his two controversial Post-Impressionist Exhibitions, in 1910 and 1912 and, secondly, by presenting him with Vanessa, whose own marriage had reached a crisis by 1911. His involvement with Vanessa in turn brought him into close contact with Virginia.

In her usual fanciful, but perceptive way, Virginia compared Roger to some wonderful red-tinted sea-anemone, 'which lives in the deepest water and sucks in to itself every scrap of living matter within miles'. His mind she thought far subtler and more richly stocked than the other art critic of the group, Clive, who learnt a great deal from Roger. Virginia believed Roger to be the only really 'civilized' man she had ever met. As a critic of her own work, she found him very honest, even brutally frank at times. Yet she respected the purity of

intellect which had led to the frankness and benefited
from his criticism. For harsh as it could be, his criticism
was always highly creative, like Roger himself. 'Why do
you always compound "intelligence" with destructive
criticism?' she asked a friend in 1935, the year after
Roger's death. 'Roger, who was the most intelligent of
my friends was profusely, ridiculously, perpetually
creative: couldn't see two matches without making them
into a boat. That was the secret of his charm and genius'.

While Roger was alive, Virginia joked about wanting
to write the obituary of such an interesting man. After
his death, however, she found it very difficult to execute,
since it seemed to her almost impossible to convey his
vividness and charm. When she did finally succumb to
his sister's repeated pleas and produced a biography,
the result was curiously flat and dead. As a mainly
fictional writer Virginia often felt constrained by hard
fact.

Roger Fry had already mounted his first Post-Impressionist Exhibition when Leonard Woolf returned to
Bloomsbury half-way through 1911, but Leonard
became Secretary of the second Exhibition. By the time
this took place in the autumn of 1912 Leonard was also
married to Virginia. He had met her only briefly before
his departure for Ceylon, when he dined with Virginia,
Vanessa, Thoby and Adrian at 46 Gordon Square on
17 November 1904. Virginia was still recovering from
the breakdown following her father's death and Leonard
remembered her as completely silent and drawn — an 'odd
fish', as Virginia put it. She had already formed a bizarre
impression of him through the garbled stories Thoby
told her: how his hand trembled and how he was so
passionate that he had once bitten his thumb through in
a rage. Lytton added that Leonard was like Swift and
would murder his wife. After his departure for Ceylon,
the rumours continued: how he had married a black

woman and lived in a jungle. Lytton half-jokingly encouraged a romance after his own broken engagement to Virginia, by suggesting in his letters that Leonard should marry her. So that by the time he met her again on 3 July 1911, when he dined with the Bells at Gordon Square, he was already intrigued by her. Virginia, who came in after dinner with Duncan Grant and Walter Lamb, was as conscious of her unmarried state as he was and almost certainly ready to think of him as an eligible suitor.

Leonard was already in a state of flux. His excitement at being back in England was both marred and heightened by his inability to decide whether to stay, or return to Ceylon. Meeting Virginia increased both his exhilaration and indecision. It is clear that she responded to his interest in her, for in July 1911 she invited him for a weekend to Little Talland, the house she had started to rent early in the year at Firle on the Sussex downs. When Leonard took up her offer in September they immediately fell into a routine of reading and walking which must have made them both feel that they could live happily together. Leonard was not deterred by Virginia's physical coldness towards him and found himself falling in love with her. In October he invited her to share a box he had rented at Covent Garden, in honour of Wagner's *Ring* cycle. After each performance he would go back for supper with her to Fitzroy Square, which she and Adrian were about to vacate. It was not surprising, therefore, that they should ask Leonard to share their next house, Brunswick Square. He moved in on 4 December and naturally began to see even more of Virginia, who would often take her tray up to his room, or invite him down to hers. When he asked her to marry him in early January 1912, she said she needed time to think about it. Leonard, who was due to return to Ceylon soon, tried to get his leave extended. When this

failed, he resigned, preferring the possibility of a life
with Virginia to the certainty of a safe job away from
her.

Leonard resigned from the Ceylon Civil Service in
April 1912, but it was not until the end of May that
Virginia agreed to marry him. Since his proposal in
January she had had many opportunities to test her
feelings for him. Although, as she frankly told him, she
did not reciprocate his physical passion, she had begun
to 'feel half in love . . . some feeling that was permanent,
and growing'. They had spent at least two weekends a
month together at a house they had discovered near
Firle—Asham House (see pages 227-231). Set in an
isolated spot in the Ouse valley, it was far preferable to
Little Talland, which Virginia readily exchanged for it. She
and Leonard continued to take long walks together over
the Sussex downs, as they were to all their lives. So that,
when Virginia accepted him on 29 May, it was a considered act, based on a sense of compatibility. Though she
still felt no physical response to him—her feelings towards
men generally were 'all of the spiritual, intellectual,
emotional kind'—they both hoped, in vain as it turned
out, that the situation would change with marriage.
Leonard respected her honesty and accepted her reserv-
ations. It was for her mind, more than her body that he
loved her, fortunately. In his secret diary he had named
Virginia 'Aspasia', after the famous Athenian mistress
of Pericles, said to be the wisest woman of her time.

The marriage of Leonard and Virginia took place
seven weeks after her acceptance on 10 August 1912.
Meantime Leonard was taken to visit Virginia's relations,
including Thackeray's daughter, 'Aunt Anny' Ritchie,
and Virginia's cousin Will Vaughan, who had married
John Addington Symonds's daughter, Madge. George
Duckworth had also to be visited at East Grinstead,
where he lived in a grand house with his wife, Lady

Margaret Herbert. The contrast with Leonard's own
family must have struck both Leonard and Virginia.
Virginia, who had always taken her social privilege for
granted, disliked the suburbs. She also, like many of her
contemporaries, rather despised Jews. So that the visit
to Leonard's large, noisy, Jewish family in Colinette
Road, Putney, can hardly have been a success. It is
described vividly in her thinly disguised autobiography,
Night and Day, when Katharine Hilberry from Cheyne
Walk visits Ralph Denham's large, disorganised Jewish
family at Highgate. Nearly twenty years later Virginia
remembered how she had hated marrying a Jew: 'how I
hated their nasal voices, and their oriental jewellry, and
their noses and their wattles'. Yet she also realised what
a snob she had been and grew to appreciate their warmth
and vitality.

Leonard, like the rest of his family, was immensely
energetic. He was also very hard-working and pertinacious.
So that, although not as brilliant, intellectually or artistic-
ally, as most of the other members of Bloomsbury, he
achieved as much if not more than they. It was his
energy and industry which turned the Hogarth Press,
for instance, from a small amateur venture without any
capital into a commercial success. It also made him an
ideal editor of *The Nation*, which later amalgamated
with *The New Statesman*. In addition it made him
effective in politics, where two of his main interests
were the Co-operative movement and the League of
Nations. Finally, it enabled him to write a great many
books on these and other subjects.

Like most interesting people, however, Leonard
defies simple analysis. For there were other, contradictory
sides to his nature. Virginia, who had reason to know,
always emphasized his great kindness. Through her
frequent bouts of severe depression, 'flu and other
mysterious illnesses, Leonard nursed her like a 'perfect

angel'. He cooked for her, fed her and played music to her whilst having to carry on with his own busy life. Yet his kindness was tempered by a certain severity, which made Dora Carrington christen him 'the grissily [grizzly] wolf'. He could also be very detached, which added to the impression of severity. 'He sits on the edge of my bed,' Virginia told a friend during one of her illnesses, 'and considers my symptoms like a judge'. Indeed there was something very judicious in Leonard, whom Virginia cast significantly as a lawyer in her autobiographical *Night and Day*. Leonard's own father had been a highly successful Q.C., until his early death at forty-six of tuberculosis. Leonard's paternal grandfather, from whom the family energy and pertinacity doubtless stemmed, had built up a small tailor's business to include shops in Bond Street, Regent Street and Piccadilly. By Leonard's generation the sons were automatically expected to have a university education, but with the early death of his father this was not at all easy. His mother, herself a lady of great determination, was left with nine children and very little money. Fortunately, all six sons won scholarships to St Paul's and Leonard went on to win another to Trinity College, Cambridge. So that it was something of a shock when he failed to get into the Home Civil Service at the level he wanted and had to settle for the Ceylon Civil Service instead.

Once in Ceylon Leonard began to show the judicial side of his nature, sitting in courts and arbitrating among the natives with total impartiality, so much so that he strikes one at this period as being a little in-human. In fact most of the young men who came to work for him at the Hogarth Press later found him difficult to work with for that very reason. He was as hard on them as he was on himself. Yet his firmness and strong sense of justice made him completely reliable, which was exactly what Virginia, with her instability, needed: 'so slow and sure and everlasting is he'.

Leonard might be severe, Virginia conceded, but he stimulated her to write in a way Lytton Strachey would never have done, had she married him instead. Leonard stimulated not only because he was severe; he was also imaginative. His response to Virginia, with all her problems, alone proves that. His founding of the Hogarth Press also indicates a man of imagination, particularly when one looks at the writers he published (see page 98). He also entered into the world of fantasy Virginia created round their intimacy; he played Mandril to her Mongoose and inhabited this playful animal world without self-consciousness. Though Virginia felt no strong physical attraction to him, she got 'exquisite pleasure' merely from holding his hand. On the rare occasions when he went away she missed him intensely and wrote to him daily. They had no children, on the advice of Virginia's doctors, but they had a family of pets, a marmoset among them. It was a very intimate life they shared and one which Virginia needed to spark her imagination. Leonard made the world dance for her, gave her a sense of what she called 'fanning and drumming', as well as a sense of unity and coherence. Without this perpetual stimulation she could not write. On a more practical level Leonard also helped her to write by encouraging her through her frequent doubts and depressions. Without him, she told a friend in 1930, she would have shot herself a long time before. There were times when she felt guilty at the trouble she caused him; she saw herself as a 'curse' and a 'burden'. For the most part, however, she felt that no one could be happier than Leonard and Virginia Woolf.

13 Clifford's Inn (1912-1913)

Happiness did not come all at once for Leonard and

5. *13 Clifford's Inn*, off Fleet
Street: the flat Virginia and
Leonard found for themselves
after their marriage in 1912.

Virginia. There were problems at the beginning of their married life. On their long honeymoon through France, Spain and Italy they discovered that Virginia was as sexually frigid as they had both feared. When they returned home there was the problem of accommodation, since neither of them wished to start married life with communal living at Brunwick Square. As in previous moves, Virginia wanted to be near, but not too near to Gordon Square, a sentiment which Leonard shared. Their choice was also limited by finance, since Leonard had only a temporary job as Roger Fry's Secretary at the Second Post-Impressionist Exhibition and Virginia her legacy. The City seemed a possibility. Both of them loved the bustle and hum of weekday life there and the almost eerily quiet weekends. For Leonard it brought back memories of his father, who had taken him as a child to visit his chambers at 7 King's Bench Walk. For Virginia it represented the serious, working side to life, as compared with the frivolity and superficiality of the West End. When Elizabeth, in *Mrs Dalloway*, takes the bus from Westminster to Fleet Street, she is symbolically escaping from her hostess-mother's world.

Virginia was particularly fond of Fleet Street and the maze of narrow streets surrounding it, partly because it was the centre of journalism, partly because it led to St Paul's at one end and the Law Courts at the other. She was, therefore, delighted when they found rooms at 13 Clifford's Inn, a small court sandwiched between Chancery and Fetter Lane, just a few yards from Fleet Street itself. Clifford's Inn was still then the old building, not the rather functional block which replaced it and which has recently been refurbished. Virginia is almost certainly referring to the old Clifford's Inn when she describes William Rodney's flat in *Night and Day*:

They [i.e. William and his friend, Ralph Denham] had

reached a small court of high eighteenth-century houses, in one of which Rodney had his rooms. They climbed a very steep staircase, through whose uncurtained windows the moonlight fell, illuminating the banisters with their twisted pillars, and the piles of plates set on the window-sills, and jars half-full of milk. Rodney's rooms were small, but the sitting-room window looked out into a courtyard with its flagged pavement, and its single tree, and across to the flat red-brick fronts of the opposite houses, which would not have surprised Dr Johnson, if he had come out of his grave for a turn in the moonlight.

Leonard also thought of Dr Johnson and others at Clifford's Inn. With Fleet Street, the Temple, Fetter Lane and Gough Square on the doorstep he was constantly aware of literary associations: 'one felt it had been lived in for hundreds of years by Chaucer, Shakespeare, Pepys, Johnson, Boswell'. Leonard also tells us that their rooms were 'incredibly ancient, also incredibly draughty and dirty'. In spite of this, Virginia thought them delightful. She also appreciated the little patch of green in the court below as a possible children's playground. For she was still expecting to have children, though Leonard was already beginning to wonder whether she could cope with the experience. (It is sad now to think of her slightly embarrassed pleasure when she saw the beautiful old cradle Violet Dickinson had bought her as a wedding present.)

Meantime, she and Leonard settled down to a life together, dining at the Cock Tavern in Fleet Street, taking long walks east further into the City and shorter walks north-west to visit Bloomsbury friends. They also entertained occasional visitors in their tiny flat, such as Margaret Llewelyn Davies with whom Leonard had begun work in the Women's Co-operative Guild. The 'Woolves', as their friends called them, spent most of the day writing, for Virginia was at last finishing *The Voyage Out*, which had started as *Melymbrosia* in Fitzroy Square five years earlier. Leonard, who still hoped to earn a living by writing, was starting a new novel, *The Wise Virgins*, having just completed his story on Ceylon, *The Village in the Jungle*. It is pleasing to picture them both, as Leonard paints them, sitting writing by their open windows, while a 'thin veil of smuts covered the page' they were engaged on.

Their happiness was short-lived. The effort of finishing *The Voyage Out* and the fear of exposing it, and herself, to criticism, combined with the strains of being newly married led Virginia to one of the worst breakdowns of her life. After her novel had been accepted by her half-brother Gerald's firm of Duckworth in April 1913, she began to have sleepless nights, followed by severe headaches. She was gradually overwhelmed by depression, a sense of guilt and an aversion to food, until she could bear it no longer. On 9 September 1913, she took an overdose of her sleeping draught, veronal, and would certainly have died had not Leonard acted very promptly. Once she was out of danger he decided to move her from London, which he thought far too stimulating for one of her extreme sensitivity. Her other half-brother, George Duckworth, very kindly insisted that she should recuperate at Dalingridge, his large country house, and she remained there with Leonard and two nurses until mid-November. By this time she was well enough to be moved to their own country house, Asham, where she spent the next nine months under the care of two old friends, Janet Case and Ka Cox. In December 1913 Leonard moved their belongings from Clifford's Inn, to which Virginia never returned.

17 The Green, Richmond, Surrey (1914-1915)

It was as a direct result of Virginia's breakdown in 1913 that Leonard decided to move out of central London. When, after a year in the country, she was ready to return to something like normality, it was not the hectic, highly stimulating life of Bloomsbury or the City. Instead Leonard insisted that they live somewhere quieter, less intense in the suburbs. Virginia, who had always hated the suburbs, had nevertheless to agree. Indeed she was happy to agree. Even she could see the need for calm and rest. At least she would be within commuting distance of her beloved London. So would Leonard, who had become increasingly involved in political work, particularly the Women's Co-operative Guild at Hampstead. Perhaps Leonard felt that Hampstead itself was too near to Bloomsbury, for he rejected both it and Highgate in favour of Richmond. Clustered on and around a large hill to the south-west of London, Richmond is virtually encircled by the river Thames, which curves round on its way from Kew to Kingston. Leonard probably chose Richmond not only for its beauty but also because of its nearness to Putney, where his widowed mother lived. Though intensely critical of his family in general, he was a devoted and dutiful son, often to the exasperation of Virginia. Most of Leonard's filial visits were performed alone.

Virginia and Leonard moved into lodgings at 17 The Green, Richmond on 16 October 1914. Virginia took an immediate liking to Richmond; it seemed to her that it was not an offshoot of London, which was what made most suburbs so dull, but a small town in itself. It was only a short journey by tube or train from the nearby station to central London. Virginia must have taken the district line to Sloane Square many times, as the faithful

6. *17 The Green, Richmond, Surrey*: the lodgings Virginia and Leonard occupied after the first stage of Virginia's fourth nervous breakdown, in 1913.

old servant Crosby does in her novel *The Years*. Equally
near, for walks with her dog, Max, was the vast Old Deer
Park, which bordered on Kew Gardens to the north and
Syon Park to the west. Running through and round all
three was the Thames, which provided other favourite
walks, though there were times when flooding prevented
these. A little further to the south lay Richmond Hill
and Richmond Park, another large expanse of beautiful
country for her to walk in. If she wanted more cultural
pursuits Hampton Court and Ham House were not far away.

For more practical purposes the main shopping area
was only a few yards away from the Woolfs' lodgings. In
fact 17 The Green backed on to the shops. In the days
before the motor car became common, however, Richmond Green was a peaceful and beautiful place to live.
The houses were substantial and Leonard and Virginia
had a large first-floor drawing room overlooking the
Green itself. Their house was distinguished from its
neighbours by a pointed attic room at the front, with a
Dutch gable not unlike 22 Hyde Park Gate. It was kept
by a Belgian woman, Mrs Le Grys, an 'extremely nice
plump excitable flibbertigibbet, about 35 to 40', according to Leonard. Virginia would 'interview' Mrs Le Grys
every morning after breakfast about their meals for the
day and she found their landlady quite entertaining,
particularly when she related stories about the grossness
of Belgian appetites. Virginia and Leonard would then
settle down to their 'scribbling', for Virginia had
been allowed to start writing again. After lunch, a read
of the newspapers and a rest for Virginia, they would
normally take Max for a walk, either to the park or the
river. Virginia would then shop and return home for a
tea of bread, honey and cream. The evening would be
spent reading by the fire. Number 17 The Green still
stands, unchanged externally from Virginia's day, except
for the unfortunate introduction of a tradesman's

entrance in place of one of the ground-floor windows.

Hogarth House, Richmond, Surrey (1915-1924)

For four months the Woolfs' cosy routine at 17 The
Green continued, broken only by occasional days in
London, when Leonard would see about some political
or journalistic matter and Virginia would shop, renew
her library books, attend concerts or visit friends. Meantime they were looking for a house of their own to rent
and in December 1914 they found one. Only a short
walk across Richmond's main square, Hogarth House
was situated half-way along Paradise Road, a name that
must surely have appealed to Virginia. Hogarth was the
right-hand part of the original Suffield House, which
had been divided into two. Built by Lord Suffield in
1720, it was classically Georgian, with an elegant central
porch, divided between two doors by 1914, and sym-
metrical sash windows. Its mellow red bricks have since
been painted at basement level, the windows replaced
and the basement, ground and upper floor turned into
offices, but it is still possible to imagine how it must
have looked when the Woolfs first saw it. Every room
but one, Leonard tells us, was perfectly proportioned.
He does not tell us which the exception was. Virginia's
response was less architectural; she found it 'rather nice,
shabby, ancient, very solid'. They both loved the garden,
which was almost 100 ft long and therefore large enough
for both vegetables and flowers. After prolonged negot-
iations they finally obtained a lease on Hogarth House
and were due to move in in March 1915.
   Then, quite suddenly in the middle of February,
Virginia fell ill again. It was the beginning of the second
stage of her mental breakdown, which was even more
terrifying than the first. So that when March came

7. *Hogarth House, Paradise Road, Richmond, Surrey*:
Virginia and Leonard moved into the right of these two
houses during the second stage of Virginia's nervous
breakdown in 1915. They started the Hogarth Press in
the dining-room here in 1917. They eventually also took
over the lease of the left-hand dwelling, Suffield House,
just before they left in 1924.

Leonard had to move into Hogarth House single-handed with four mental nurses to control Virginia. As her violence subsided, the number of nurses was reduced until by the end of the year the last one had gone. Strangely enough, Virginia loved Hogarth House partly *because* she had spent the first nine months there insane:

> I've had some very curious visions in this room [she wrote as she was leaving it] . . . lying in bed, mad, and seeing the sunlight quivering like gold water, on the wall. I've heard the voices of the dead here. And felt, through it all, exquisitely happy.

Leonard believed that the main reason Virginia's health periodically broke down was her tendency to overwork, particularly on her fiction. He felt he might prevent this by providing her with an interesting manual occupation, such as printing. He was also genuinely interested in learning to print himself. They had been on the point of buying a small hand-press when Virginia became ill in February 1915, but it was not until March 1917 that they finally got it. By this time it was even more necessary to provide Virginia with a distraction from writing, for she was working harder than ever. Apart from regular reviewing for *The Times Literary Supplement*, she had started a second novel, *Night and Day*, and was experimenting with short pieces like 'The Mark on the Wall'.

Leonard and Virginia bought their small hand-press on an impulse one afternoon when walking up Farringdon Street from Fleet Street to Holborn Viaduct. The Excelsior Printing Supply Company provided them not only with a printing machine, type, chases and other vital equipment, but also a sixteen-page pamphlet teaching them how to print, all for £19 5s 5d.* When the press

*This is about £19.25 p. new money.

was delivered to Hogarth House, the only place they could find for it was the dining-room, where it remained for the rest of their stay. Virginia's invitation to Vita Sackville-West in 1923 has become well-known: 'We don't dine so much as picnic, as the press has got into the larder and the dining-room . . .' It not only ousted them from the dining-room, but crept all over the house, making everything, according to Virginia, 'incredibly untidy'.

After a month's practice Leonard and Virginia felt confident enough to attempt their first production — *Two Stories*, by themselves. Virginia's was 'The Mark on the Wall', Leonard's 'Three Jews'. They also 'bound' their edition of 150 copies by simply stitching the pages into paper covers. Encouraged by the response, they went on to publish *Prelude* by Katherine Mansfield in 1918, *Poems* by T.S. Eliot, *Kew Gardens* by Virginia and *The Critic in Judgement* by John Middleton Murry in 1919 and *The Story of the Siren* by E.M. Forster in 1920. With such a gifted group of friends to call on, it is not surprising that the Hogarth Press quickly developed into a successful commercial venture.

The Hogarth Press was only one of many activities at Hogarth House. Once Virginia was sufficiently recovered she began to want to invite friends there. As usual, Leonard felt he must moderate her impulses, which were generally excessive, but he agreed to a certain amount of entertainment. Visitors were invited either to lunch or dinner and the privileged ones sometimes stayed the night. Virginia's former Greek teacher, Janet Case, often came and her old friend Ka Cox, so did Leonard's colleague in the Women's Co-operative Guild, Margaret Llewelyn Davies. Bloomsbury frequently came in the form of Clive Bell, Maynard Keynes, Saxon Sydney-Turner, Sydney Waterlow, Desmond MacCarthy, Lytton Strachey, Walter Lamb and, occasionally, Vanessa, who

was now living with Duncan Grant. Less congenially to
Virginia, Leonard's large family also visited, though they
were rarely asked to stay the night. Lady Ottoline
Morrell, having renewed her friendship with Virginia,
paid them memorable visits and issued numerous invitations to her country house, Garsington. Even the
elusive Morgan Forster came 'like a vaguely rambling
butterfly' and other writers arrived in the interests of
the Hogarth Press.

One of the most notable of these was T.S. Eliot, who
gradually became a close friend. When Leonard first met
Eliot in 1917, he was not yet an established poet, having
had only *Prufrock* published by the Egoist Press that
same year. Eliot was still working at Lloyd's Bank,
though he also helped run the *Egoist* magazine in his
spare time. And there was something of the bank clerk
about him, Leonard felt, with his precise, rather formal,
cautious, even inhibited manner. Virginia, who met him
a year later when he first visited Hogarth House, found
'a polished, cultivated, elaborate young American, talking so slow that each word seemed to have special finish
allotted it'. Beneath this surface, however, she saw that
he was 'very intellectual, intolerant, with strong views
of his own, and a poetic creed'. She never changed her
mind about the force of Eliot's intellect, though she did
find him far less formal and pedantic as she got to know
him. The ice was broken during a weekend he spent at
their country house, which all three thoroughly enjoyed.
'Tom', as they called him, was grateful to them for
publishing seven of his poems in 1919. They also went
on to publish the first edition in England of his most
famous and controversial work, *The Waste Land*, in 1923.

Another writer Virginia got to know during the
Hogarth House period was Katherine Mansfield.
Katherine and her future husband, John Middleton
Murry, were very sympathetic towards the Hogarth Press

venture. When Leonard and Virginia were looking around
for something to follow their own *Two Stories* in 1917,
Katherine offered her short story *Prelude*, which became
their second publication. It was a courageous undertak-
ing for beginners, since it ran to 68 pages, which Virginia
set by hand and Leonard machined at a nearby friendly
printers. They sold 257 of their edition of 300 copies,
but the real importance of the event for Virginia was
the beginning of her friendship with Katherine. Though
their backgrounds were quite different—Katherine was a
New Zealander and already separated from her first
husband by 1917—they had a great deal in common.
They both loved writing. Virginia found with Katherine
something she missed in other clever women, 'a sense of
ease and interest', which she felt came from her caring
'so genuinely if so differently' about their 'precious art'.
In spite of Katherine's success, she was 'not the least of
a hack'. Virginia could also identify, at a quite different
level, with Katherine's constant fight against ill-health.
Yet as her tuberculosis grew worse the relationship grew
more unreal to Virginia, who only afterwards realised
that Katherine had not been detaching herself from
Virginia, but from life itself. To begin with Virginia had
grown to like Katherine increasingly, but, as the New
Zealander became successful, Virginia became more
critical, partly out of jealousy she later admitted. She
began to find a cheapness and sentimentality in both
Katherine and her writings. Yet in retrospect it was
Katherine's 'zest and resonance', her 'sharpness and
reality' that she both admired and needed.

Shortly after meeting Katherine in 1917 Virginia had
written: 'Friendships with women interest me' and her
most passionate relationships do seem to have been with
women. The most important of these, apart from her
intense love of Vanessa, also had its roots in Hogarth
House. For it was here that she first met another woman

writer, who was to fascinate and exasperate her even
more than Katherine—Vita Sackville-West.

Virginia first met Vita, the daughter of Lord Sackville
of Knole, through Clive Bell, who shared his sister-in-
law's fascination with the aristocracy. After dinner with
Vita and her diplomat husband, Harold Nicholson, at
the end of 1922, Virginia met her with increasing
frequency in 1923 and 1924. It was not until 1925,
however, when Vita was due to visit Harold in Persia,
that she realised how strongly she felt about her 'lovely'
aristocrat. Unlike Katherine Mansfield, she did not
admire Vita for her writing, though the Hogarth Press
was to benefit from Vita's undoubted talents which sold
her books by the thousands. It was rather in spite of
what Virginia called Vita's 'pen of brass' that she admired
her. Virginia freely admitted to her own snobbishness
and it was first and foremost Vita's aristocracy that appealed to her. (Vita herself, with inverted snobbery, was
always anxious to emphasize the humbler parts of her
origins.) Even Vita's appearance seemed to Virginia to
reflect her privileged background:

> I like her and being with her and the splendour—she
> shines in the grocer's shop in Sevenoaks with candle
> lit radiance, stalking on legs like beech [birch?] trees,
> pink glowing, grape clustered, pearl hung.

Virginia loved Vita's romantic strain, which thrived at
her ancestral home, Knole, with its ancient buildings,
vast parklands and nightingales. More than that, she
found Vita what she felt she could never be herself, a
'real woman'. Though she thought Vita a rather cold
mother to her two sons, Virginia got from her the maternal protection she needed in those closest to her, Vanessa
and Leonard in particular. With Vita she chose to be
another small animal in need of protection, a 'potto',

the monkey-like African lemur. Vita was her 'insect', though it is difficult to see why Virginia chose such a humble creature for her far from insignificant friend. For Vita had a certain majesty about her which could be daunting.

One strong contrast Virginia found with herself was Vita's physical passion, especially for women. She loved the story of Vita's elopement with her cousin, Violet Trefusis, to some mountainous retreat and hoped that her 'adorable, dusky, tortured, passionate' friend would choose her next. Yet when Vita made physical advances, Virginia's first impulse was to retreat. Vita, like Clive, called her a cold fish, but Virginia explained, as she had to Leonard, that she was not a very physical person. A mere touch of the hand, of either man or woman, could give her exquisite pleasure. Nevertheless she did respond physically to Vita, who broke down more ramparts she told her, than anyone else. The main appeal in the relationship for Virginia, however, was the sense of illusion Vita created and which Virginia needed to make life 'vibrate'. It was the 'festival and the firelight' rather than the lovemaking that entranced her. In moments of disillusion with Vita, when Vita accused her of looking on all relationships as copy, for example, Virginia accused her aristocrat of lacking 'vibration'. Both were to some extent right. Vita did not share Virginia's intense response to life and Virginia did indeed make copy of her relationships. Even while her friendship with Vita was at its height from 1925 to 1927, she was planning and writing *Orlando*, which was based almost entirely on her experience of Vita. (Vita's ambiguous sexuality, for instance, is reflected in Orlando's actual change of sex in the novel.) It was not so much, as Vita argued, that Virginia approached people through her brain rather than her heart, but that her 'heart' lay in her writing.

Although Virginia's passion for Vita died down quite

quickly, she kept her appreciation of her character. In
writing to a mutual friend in 1935, Virginia shows that
her satiric gift is not confined to her fictional characters,
even towards those she genuinely loves:

> Then Vita came; and you'll be amused to hear that
> though my love of her character, so modest so mag-
> nanimous, remains unimpaired, I cant really forgive
> her for growing so large: with such tomato cheeks
> and thick black moustache — Surely that wasn't neces-
> sary: and the devil is that it shuts up her eyes that
> were the beaming beauty I first loved her for, and
> altogether reduces her (to look at) to the semblance
> of any fox hunting turnip stalking country lady.

52 Tavistock Square (1924-1939)

Virginia's relationship with Vita had started while she
was living at Hogarth House, but it was played out
against a very different background. For at least five
years Virginia had appreciated 'dipping' in to London
and returning to the 'purer air' of Richmond. Nowhere,
she felt, could have suited her better during the years
following her breakdown, when she was 'creeping about
like a rat struck on the head' and the war was devastating central London. As she grew stronger, however, she
began to feel like an exile away from her true home.
Though by 1923 she and Leonard had bought the lease
of Suffield House, the other half to Hogarth, by the
middle of that year she was convinced they must leave
Richmond. At the same time she doubted whether
Leonard would ever allow her to return to the excitement of living in central London. Yet it was precisely
that stimulation she now needed for her work, which
with the completion of *Night and Day* in 1919 and

Jacob's Room in 1922, was becoming increasingly experimental. Richmond did not stimulate her to further
daring. Nowhere does she so clearly declare the relationship between her work and London and between 'life'
and London than in the following passage written in
1923:

This may be life; but I doubt that I shall ever convert
L[eonard] and now sit down baffled and depressed to
face a life spent, mute and mitigated in the suburbs,
just as I had it in mind that I could at last go full
speed ahead. For the capacities in me will never after
40, accumulate again. And I mind missing life far
more than he does, for it isn't life to him in the sense
that it is life to me. Oh to be able to slip in and out
of things easily, to be in them, not on the verge of
them—I resent this effort and waste . . . oh to dwindle
out [our short years of life] here, with all these gaps
and abbreviations! Always to catch trains, always to
waste time, to sit here and wait for Leonard to come
in . . . when, alternatively, I might go and hear a tune,
or have a look at a picture, or find out something in
the British Museum, or go adventuring among human
beings. Sometimes I should merely walk down Cheap-
side. But now I'm tied, imprisoned, inhibited . . . For
ever to be suburban. L[eonard] I don't think minds
any of this as much as I do . . . There is, I suppose, a
very different element in us; my social side, his intellectual side. This social side is very genuine in me. Nor
do I think it reprehensible. It is a piece of jewellery I
inherit from my mother—a joy in laughter, something
that is stimulated not selfishly wholly or vainly, by
contact with my friends. And then ideas leap in me.
Moreover for my work now, I want freer intercourse,
wider intercourse . . .

8. *52 Tavistock Square, Blooms-bury*: the house where Virginia wrote most of her greatest novels which were published by the Hogarth Press in the basement.

When in October 1923 Leonard reluctantly agreed to move, Virginia became so excited that it must have confirmed his worst fears. She rushed up to London immediately and began house-hunting. By November she had found a house at 35 Woburn Square. When this fell through she discovered the house they were to live in for the next fifteen years—52 Tavistock Square. On 9 January 1924 they signed a ten-year lease and, on 13 March, moved in. After the 'softness' of Richmond's parks and rivers, Virginia found Bloomsbury 'fierce and scornful and stonyhearted' but nevertheless incredibly beautiful. This beauty lay in its vitality, for it seemed to her pulsing with life. Marchmont Street was like Paris, the moon was brighter and more terrifying, the streets were swarming with strangers. London had an oddity and character that Richmond lacked: Richmond was, she concluded, 'all very well for Americans'! On a more practical level she appreciated having more time to read and not having to rush to catch the last train home, as well as seeing more of Leonard. She missed her walks in Richmond Park, Kew Gardens and by the river, but there was Regent's Park not far away to console her.

The house itself also seemed to Virginia very exciting, partly because of its outlook. Situated on the south side of Tavistock Square, number 52 had a view not only of the large communal garden in the centre of the square but also of the carved white spire of St Pancras Church and pink and blue Imperial Hotel in Russell Square. Virginia loved watching the buses pass up and down Southampton Row, though curiously enough she found them less noisy than the distant buses in Fitzroy Square. (Later on there were problems with noise from a neighbouring hotel.) Gordon Square was only a few hundred yards to the west, but after years of exile Virginia was no longer anxious to keep her distance from it. She could not now be near enough. Gordon Square was fuller than it had ever

been of 'Bloomsberries', as they came jokingly to be
called. Clive had a flat in Adrian Stephen's house at
number 50, Vanessa was renting number 37, which she
shared with Duncan when they were not in Sussex or
France. Maynard was at number 46 with Lydia Lopokova,
whom he married in 1925. Lytton's brother, James,
shared number 41 with Alix Sargant Florence. He also
let a flat to Ralph Partridge to use during the week with
Frances Marshall. (At weekends Ralph returned to Ham
Spray, where his wife, Dora Carrington, was living with
her real love, Lytton.) Slightly further west at 10 Gower
Street Lady Ottoline Morrell moved back into London
from Garsington in 1927. To the east was Saxon Sydney-
Turner in a flat at 37 Great Ormond Street.

Like many of the houses in this area, 52 Tavistock
Square was part of an early nineteenth-century terrace
with four floors and a basement. It had the usual wrought
iron railings but, unlike Gordon Square, its brickwork
was unrendered. The house and terrace, after severe
bomb damage in the Second World War, have since been
demolished and the site is now occupied by the Tavistock
Hotel.

Leonard rented only the basement and top two floors
of number 52, the ground and first floor being already
leased to a firm of solicitors, Dolman and Pritchard. The
basement was given over almost entirely to the expand-
ing Hogarth Press, which grew even more vigorously in
its spacious new premises. Leonard continued to look for
suitable young people to help. These younger people
tended to be given the more menial tasks of invoicing and
packing in far from comfortable conditions. One Hogarth
Press employee, John Lehmann, who eventually bought
out Virginia's share in the enterprise, remembered the
basement at number 52 as cold, draughty and ramshackle,
piled high with dusty files and packets of books. But he
also felt, like all the young people who went to work

there, that there was glamour and excitement attached
to working for Leonard and Virginia.

Lehmann was particularly thrilled to be sent to
Virginia's studio, where most of the stock was kept.
Though not quite a 'room of [her] own', shared as it was
with mountains of books, Virginia did most of her
writing there.

Away from the main activity of the Press, down a
long passage at the back of the basement, this room
became a 'holy of holies'. Originally a billiard room
built under the garden, it had a skylight which gave it an
underwater feel and added to its sense of mystery. On
arriving at Tavistock Square Virginia began enthusiastically
to furnish this room with a piece of matting bought
cheaply from Hammonds, a rug, a table, a bed, a book-
case, an old armchair and some artificial flowers and
pictures provided by Vanessa. Here Virginia would sit,
when her health allowed it, writing her statutory three
hours every morning. Having finished *Jacob's Room* at
Hogarth House in 1922, in 1924 she was hard at work on
Mrs Dalloway, which came out in 1925. It may well have
been the stimulation of returning to London which helped
her to produce one of her finest novels in her first year
back there. (*Mrs Dalloway* is located almost entirely in
central London.) Certainly it was Tavistock Square itself
which sparked off her next novel, *To the Lighthouse*.
Though this is set in the Hebrides, it is a thinly disguised
evocation of her childhood holidays in Cornwall. When
To the Lighthouse was published in 1927, and Virginia
was already beginning to plan *Orlando* and *The Waves*,
she reflected on the 'odd hurried way in which these
things suddenly create themselves — one thing on top of
another in about an hour. So I made up *Jacob's Room*
looking at the fire in Hogarth House, so I made up *The
Lighthouse* one afternoon in the square here'.

Virginia also enjoyed the garden square in less elevated

ways, walking her dog and chatting to friends, Vanessa
in particular, there. When she had finished her morning's
work she would climb the stairs past two floors of
solicitors to the flat she and Leonard had made for themselves on the second and third storeys. Here, after lunch,
she might work on something lighter, such as a review,
but from four o'clock onwards she generally entertained
friends. For this purpose she had created a drawing-room,
decorated by Vanessa and Duncan 'with vast panels of
moonrises and prima donna's bouquets'. Virginia had
had to force Leonard into the 'outrageous extravagance
of £25' for this. Vanessa had also designed the painted
table and pink, black and cream china in the dining-
room. Stephen Spender, who spent a number of evenings
at 52 Tavistock Square as a young man, remembered the
dining room as a lighter, perhaps more successful room
than the drawing-room. Nevertheless it is the drawing-
room he describes most vividly:

> Their drawing-room was large, tall, pleasant, square-
> shaped, with rather large and simple furniture, giving
> . . . an impression of greys and greens. Painted panels
> by Duncan Grant and Vanessa Bell represented
> mandolins, fruit, and perhaps a view of the Mediter-
> ranean through an open window or a curtain drawn
> aside. These were painted thickly and opaquely in
> browns and terracottas, reds and pale blue, with a
> hatch work effect in the foreground with shadows of
> the folds of a curtain.

In this drawing-room Virginia frequently entertained her
old Bloomsbury friends and, during 1925, 1926 and
1927, Vita Sackville-West too. Later on in the same room
she also began to see a great deal of another 'Sapphic',
as she euphemistically called lesbians, Ethel Smyth.
    Ethel, who was seventy-one when they first met in

February 1930, was a striking woman, a composer who
struggled all her life for recognition of her by no means
easy operas and orchestral pieces. She was also a prolific
writer, mainly of her own memoirs. Virginia had read
most of Ethel's works, which she admired, partly because
they were so different from her own. She had also attended at least two performances of Ethel's music before
meeting her and described her striding up the gangway
in coat and skirt and spats and talking at the top of her
voice.

For Ethel was a General's daughter and often behaved
like a soldier herself. At their first meeting, engineered
by Ethel, who was in ecstasies over Virginia's feminist
stand in *A Room of One's Own*, the General's daughter
had burst into the drawing-room in a tricorn hat and
tailored suit and poured out endless questions until
Virginia managed to get rid of her at 7.30 p.m. The
General's daughter, Virginia theorised on further acquaintance, was 'deadly shrewd, caustic, rational, severe'. Yet
she also recognised a more metaphysical side to Ethel,
an intuitive, perceptive streak which made her a fascinating companion. This enabled Ethel to see Virginia fairly
realistically, in spite of her infatuation with her. One of
Virginia's main faults, Ethel felt, was her self-absorption.

Ethel's criticism of Virginia highlights, ironically, her
own worst fault. She was extremely egotistical and very
tenacious. Virginia, with her instinct for metaphor,
thought of Ethel as a giant crab and Ethel's persistence
often led to stormy disagreements. Yet the other side of
Ethel's flamboyance was an extroversion and generosity
which Virginia valued: 'I find your atmosphere full of
ozone; a necessary element', she wrote to Ethel almost a
year after their first meeting; 'since in my set they never
praise me and never love me openly; and I admit there are
times when silence chills and the other thing fires . . .'
Virginia also found in Ethel that maternal protection she

looked for in close relationships. If Ethel could be so outspoken, she comforted herself, there was less to fear in life. It was Ethel's lack of inhibition, a complement to Virginia's own inhibitedness that finally made their relationship work. When anyone else would have been put off by Virginia's periodic rebuffs, Ethel came bouncing back for more.

This friendship with a deaf, ageing megalomaniac might seem to Virginia at times 'hideous and horrid and melancholy-sad', yet it persisted throughout the thirties. For in spite of all Ethel's faults she was, in Virginia's words, 'a game old Bird' and she respected her. More importantly for posterity, she found it easier to confide in Ethel than in any other correspondent during this period and her letters to Ethel are full of revelations about past experiences.

At a less intense level Virginia also made friends with several interesting young men during her years at Tavistock Square, mainly through the work of the Hogarth Press. Since the press had started to develop at Hogarth House there had been problems finding the right people to help. To begin with Leonard had tried women assistants, such as Alix Sargant Florence, who walked out on her first day, and Barbara Hiles, who was willing but lacked initiative. Marjorie Joad moved with the press from Hogarth House to Tavistock Square but by this time Leonard felt that a young man might be better able to cope with the ever-increasing work. George ('Dadie') Rylands, a protégé of Maynard's from Cambridge, came to help, while waiting to have his Fellowship awarded. He got on well with Virginia and brought her into contact with a younger set of intellectuals, F.L. Lucas, Raymond Mortimer and Lord David Cecil among them. When Dadie left at the end of 1924, his place was taken by another charming young friend from Cambridge, Angus Davidson. After a somewhat stormy two years,

Angus also left, unable to cope with Leonard's just but exacting demands. During the next three years Leonard and Virginia periodically considered giving up the press, which took up a great deal of their time. They put off the decision once again when John Lehmann, a Cambridge friend of Vanessa's son Julian, came to help them in 1930. Virginia's response to Lehmann was immediate: 'a tight acquiline boy, pink, with the adorable curls of youth; yes, but persistent, sharp'. With this sharp young man, who was a close friend of W.H. Auden, Stephen Spender, C. Day Lewis and Christopher Isherwood, Virginia began to discuss modern poetry, which she found nearly as alien as the public were finding her own experiments in fiction. These discussions resulted, at Lehmann's suggestion, in an interested pamphlet addressed to him by Virginia, *Letter to a Young Poet*. They also brought the group of young Left-wing poets into contact with the Hogarth Press, which published some of their works. Lehmann himself left the press after less than two years, but returned in 1937 to buy Virginia out of her share in the business, an arrangement which did not work smoothly.

Important as all these contacts were to Virginia at Tavistock Square, her real interest as at almost all other times and places in her life, lay in her writing. And the years 1924 to 1939 saw some of her best work. After *Mrs Dalloway* in 1925, *To the Lighthouse* in 1927 and *Orlando* in 1928, Virginia went on to write her most experimental and possibly her finest novel, *The Waves* in 1931. This was followed in 1936 by a less difficult, chronicle novel *The Years*, which was based on a feminist essay she had written. She also produced another feminist piece, *A Room of One's Own* in 1929 and, in a lighter vein, *Flush*, the supposed autobiography of Elizabeth Barret Browning's spaniel. Meantime she was still reviewing and writing for a number of English and American

magazines and in 1925 and 1932 the Hogarth Press published two volumes of these and other pieces, *The Common
Reader*, first and second series. So that the apparently
uneventful years at Tavistock Square, untouched by
serious depressions or breakdowns, were for her full of
excitement and discovery.

They were also years full of success. For, with the
publication of *Orlando* in 1928, Virginia had at last
become a best-selling writer. Not only did this give her
the recognition she quite naturally craved, but it also gave
her and the Hogarth Press more money. This, in turn,
meant more freedom. With their first appreciable profits,
she and Leonard bought a car, a second-hand Singer.
They also travelled more widely, visiting France, Italy,
Greece, Ireland, Holland and Germany. On one occasion
they drove their car to the South of France to visit
Vanessa and Duncan, who had taken to spending half the
year at Cassis. Such was her love of France that Virginia
wanted to buy a house there. She even went so far as to
furnish one near Cassis, but Leonard was not keen and
the venture collapsed. Instead they would take motoring
tours through France and come back enthusing about
the food and wine and landscape. More money also meant
a slightly less austere life-style, with more wine and a little
more warmth, though they never by any standards became
sybarites.

Success also brought its problems as well as its benefits.
There were an ever-increasing number of people who
wanted to visit Virginia at Tavistock Square and, while
she loved company, she feared it too. For one thing it
was difficult to work as intensely as she needed at a new
book. Too many visitors also exhausted her, as Leonard
had anticipated. Yet too much solitude depressed her.
She needed the stimulation of London, but she then needed somewhere quiet to work out the ideas that stimulation
produced. During the Tavistock Square years she and

Leonard achieved an almost perfect balance. They would
spend the week in town and many weekends and the
whole summer in the country.

By 1924 they were no longer renting Asham House.
When in 1919 the owner had refused to renew the lease
further, they had found a quite different house not far
from Firle—Monk's House at Rodmell (see page 235).

On arriving at Monk's House for the summer, Virginia
would experience intense peace. 'Often down here,' she
wrote in 1928, 'I have entered into a sanctuary; a nunnery;
had a religious retreat; of great agony once; and always
some terror: so afraid one is of loneliness: of seeing to
the bottom of the vessel. That is one of the experiences
I have had here in some Augusts; and got then to a consciousness of what I call "reality": a thing I see before
me; something abstract; but residing in the downs or sky;
beside which nothing matters; in which I shall rest and
continue to exist. Reality I call it. And I fancy sometimes this is the most necessary thing to me: that which
I seek'.

Yet Virginia realised that this rare mood of perfect
peace depended on her having been in the stir of London
for some time. It was the contrast she needed. Complain
as she might about the frenzy of city life, she depended
on it both for her personal happiness and her work.

37 Mecklenburgh Square (1939-1940)

So long as Virginia managed to preserve the balance
between London and the country, she seems to have
maintained her own precarious equilibrium. The advent
of war in 1939, however, upset that balance. When the
two houses to the east of 52 Tavistock Square were
destroyed by bombs in 1939, the Woolfs' house was
exposed to the noise of traffic from Southampton Row

and Virginia longed for a quieter home. She thought she
had found one at 37 Mecklenburgh Square, an elegant
five-storey house, with ornate entrance and cast-iron
railings slightly to the east of her old haunt in Brunswick
Square. Though the rent was rather high and there was
still the tail-end of the lease on 52 Tavistock Square to
dispose of, she longed to move there. Mecklenburgh
Square seemed 'wonderfully quiet' and very sunny compared with the war-torn Tavistock Square and she urged
Leonard to bargain for the early surrender of their lease.
Both he and their co-tenant, Mr Pritchard, talked to the
Bedford Estate accordingly. Though unsuccessful they
decided to take 37 Mecklenburgh Square, with the press
in the basement, Dolman and Pritchard the solicitors on
the ground floor and first floor and the Woolfs in a flat
at the top, as before. Virginia worried about the high
rent of £250 per annum and the unlet house in Tavistock
Square, but still managed to enjoy the spaciousness,
peacefulness and sunniness of their new flat. With her
thoughts turning more and more towards death, she even
relished the thought that they might end their lives 'looking at that great peaceful garden; in the sun'.

To begin with Virginia did indeed enjoy 37 Mecklenburgh Square, but not for long. Partly because of the
difficulties of moving in war-time London, she soon
found it generally uncomfortable: the kitchen was too
small and the other rooms, which had looked so spacious
after Tavistock Square, seemed too large, sparsely furnished as they were. In fact, she and Leonard never properly
settled in there and so it never really became a home.
Since the start of the bombing it seemed wiser to avoid
London and they installed themselves in the country at
Monk's House, visiting Mecklenburgh Square only for a
day or two every few weeks. So that when it suffered
bomb-damage in 1940 it was something of a relief to
Virginia. Leonard moved the Hogarth Press to Letch-

9. *37 Mecklenburgh Square,*
Bloomsbury: the house
Virginia and Leonard rented
when 52 Tavistock Square
became uncomfortable during
the London blitz in 1939.

worth, in Hertfordshire, and they virtually abandoned
the house. When 52 Tavistock Square was destroyed by
a bomb in October 1940, Virginia's connections with
London were almost entirely severed. At any rate she
had found war-time London a depressing experience for
the most part. To Ethel Smyth in 1940 she wrote: 'And
then the passion of my life, that is the City of London —
to see London all blasted, that too raked my heart'.
Although she admired the courage of Londoners, and
even of London herself, which she personified as a
battered but indomitable old woman 'wearing her
wounds like stars', she came to feel eventually that living
there was the life of a rat in a cage:

> You dont know what a queer place London is [she
> wrote to her niece Angelica Bell in 1939] — Here we
> are running in and out of each other's houses with
> torches and gas masks. Black night descends. Rain
> pours. Vast caterpillars are now excavating trenches
> in the Square. Shops shut at 5 or so. Many windows
> remain black all day. The streets are a hurry scurry
> of people walking. Ambulances abound. Very stout
> women wear blue trousers. No one ever sits down.
> The buses are quick but rare.

When the break with London was made final, Virginia
felt it was far more complete than any change of houses.
Though she loved Rodmell she missed London, with all
its drawbacks. 'Odd how often I think with what is love
I suppose of the City', she wrote in February 1940, 'of
the walk to the Tower; that is my England; I mean, if a
bomb destroyed one of those little alleys with the brass
bound curtains and the river smell and the old woman
reading I should feel — well, what the patriots feel'.
  Nevertheless Virginia did appreciate living wholly in
the country to begin with. Gradually, however, she

became rather restless and depressed. Partly she was worried by a new book she had started in 1939, *Between the Acts*. She was, in addition, naturally oppressed by the barbarism of war. However I also believe that she missed the stimulus of London and her friends, which might have pulled her out of her depression. As I have shown, she experienced moods of almost mystical calm at Monk's House, but often these were accompanied by intense glooms. It was as though her 'plunge into deep waters' took her too far away from the everyday world, into a region where nothing seemed to matter. Virginia found these experiences both frightening and boring, yet she felt they were of great importance: 'One goes down into the well and nothing protects one from the assault of truth. Down there I can't write or read; I exist however. I am. Then I ask myself what I am? and get a closer though less flattering answer than I should on the surface . . .'

Only at Rodmell was she alone long enough to feel like this. By her own admission it was a secluded, almost lazy life:

> Breakfast in bed. Read in bed. Bath. Order dinner. Out to Lodge.* After rearranging my room (turning table to the sun: church on right; window left; a new very lovely view) tune up, with cigarette: write till 12; stop; visit L[eonard]: look at papers; return; type till 1. Listen in [to 1 o'clock news]. Lunch. Sore jaw. Can't bite. Read papers. Walk to Southease. Back 3. Gather and arrange apples. Tea. Write a letter. Bowls. Type again. Read Michelet and write here. Cook dinner. Music. Embroidery. 9.30 read (or sleep) till 11.30. Bed.

The life she had lived in London from 1924 to 1939 had
*Her small writing hut in the garden.

been very different and in many ways very demanding:

> Three afternoons someone coming. One night, dinner
> party. Saturday a walk. Thursday shopping. Tuesday
> going to tea with Nessa. One City walk. Telephone
> ringing. L[eonard] to meetings. K[ingsley] M[artin]
> or [William] Robson bothering — that was an average
> week.

If, in London, she sank into the depths she was quickly
pulled back to the surface by the arrival of a visitor, or
an emergency in the press. So that she could not linger
in those queer regions of the mind which fascinated but
appalled her. Contrary to what Leonard had always maintained, London was good for Virginia precisely because
it kept her attached to the surface of life. What in many
people would have seemed superficial was vital to
Virginia's delicate balance. At Rodmell, particularly
once the war had started, there were few distractions
from friends or business and she sank rapidly into intro-
spection, which she began to dislike. Correspondeningly
her sense of futility, always strong, increased. Add to
that her worry over *Between the Acts* and her depression
about the war, which led to the familiar pattern of sleepless nights and headaches, and it becomes easier to
understand why she decided to end her life early in 1941.
   Leonard had begun to worry about her health at the
beginning of March that year and had persuaded her to
see Dr Octavia Wilberforce, who was also a friend, at
Brighton on 27 March. Virginia confessed to being
worried herself about her mental state; she was hearing
voices again and feared madness. She seemed reassured
by Octavia's promise of help, but not for long. The next
morning, after writing to the two people nearest to her,
Leonard and Vanessa, she walked out of the house to
the nearby River Ouse. There, with the help of a pocket-

ful of stones, she drowned herself. It was very clear from the note Leonard discovered shortly afterwards that she could no longer fight her depression:

Dearest,

I feel certain I am going mad again. I feel we can't go through another one of those terrible times. And I shan't recover this time. I begin to hear voices, and I can't concentrate. So I am doing what seems the best thing to do. You have given me the greatest possible happiness. You have been in every way all that anyone could be. I don't think two people could have been happier till this terrible disease came. I can't fight any longer. I know that I am spoiling your life, that without me you could work. And you will I know. You see I can't even write this properly. I can't read. What I want to say is I owe all the happiness of my life to you. You have been entirely patient with me and incredibly good. I want to say that—everybody knows it. If anybody could have saved me it would have been you. Everything has gone from me but the certainty of your goodness. I can't go on spoiling your life any longer.

I don't think two people could have been happier than we have been.

V.

2
The Role of London
in Virginia Woolf's Writing

Interesting as it is to look at the part London played in
Virginia's life, it is even more rewarding to explore its
role in her writing. For London is far more than a background to her novels, though it is the first and most
obvious role it plays there.

Virginia's first novel, *The Voyage Out* (1915) opens
with Mr and Mrs Ambrose walking by the Thames before
taking a cab to the port. Her second novel, *Night and Day*
(1919) is set very firmly in London. Its heroine, Katharine
Hilbery lives in Cheyne Walk, her fiancé, William Rodney,
lives near Temple Bar and his friend and rival, Ralph
Denham works nearby in Lincoln's Inn, but lives in Highgate. There are also many scenes on the Embankment,
for it is the Thames which provides a link between the
symbolic opposites of Chelsea and the City. (When
Katharine has eventually agreed to marry Ralph, one
reviewer cannot help seeing *geographical* significance in
the relationship: 'In the end of it,' he writes, 'Highgate
has come to Chelsea; raw strength to exquisite tradition.')
Virginia's third novel, *Jacob's Room* (1922) uses London
as Jacob's main room. Though the first third of the book
is set in Cornwall, Scarborough and Cambridge, the other
two-thirds are set in London, apart from an extended
description of Jacob's trip through France and Italy to
Greece. Then comes *Mrs Dalloway* (1925) which David
Daiches rightly calls '*the* London novel', rather than *The
Years*, as Dorothy Brewster claims. *Mrs Dalloway* is set
entirely in London and is Virginia's answer to James
Joyce's *Ulysses*: as he celebrates one day in the history
of Dublin, so she takes one day in the life of London.
Virginia's fifth novel, *To the Lighthouse* (1927) is set
wholly in the Hebrides, but *Orlando* (1928) has some

123

early London scenes, then switches almost completely
to London about half-way through, when Orlando
becomes a woman and returns to London from foreign
parts. Even *The Waves* (1931), abstract as it is, contains
quite sizeable passages in or about London to which
each of the six 'voices' reacts in his or her own way.
Between the Acts (1941) which was written after Virginia
had left London for good, not surprisingly contains very
few references to the capital.

In other words, London dominates the setting in *Night
and Day*, *Mrs Dalloway* and *The Years* and plays a significant part in *Jacob's Room*, *Orlando* and *The Waves*.
In *The Voyage Out* London is part of the setting, though
not a major one. Only *To the Lighthouse* and *Between
the Acts* are set completely outside London. It would
not, therefore, be difficult to illustrate many times over
London's use as a setting, though it would be harder to
show it being used simply for that purpose. The following extract does contain a few lines of pure description,
which reveal Virginia's great love of London. Mrs Ambrose
is walking with her husband near the Thames, just before
her departure for South America, but fails to see the
beauty of the scene because she is weeping at the thought
of leaving her children. The author points out:

> Sometimes the flats and churches and hotels of West-
> minster are like the outlines of Constantinople in a mist;
> sometimes the river is an opulent purple, sometimes
> mud-coloured, sometimes sparkling blue like the sea. It
> is always worth while to look down and see what is
> happening. But this lady looked neither up nor down;
> the only thing she had seen, since she stood there, was a
> circular iridescent patch slowly floating past with a straw
> in the middle of it. The straw and the patch swam again
> and again behind the tremulous medium of a great welling
> tear, and the tear rose and fell and dropped into the river.

As this passage suggests, London is very rarely used simply as a convenient setting. Here, for instance, Mrs Ambrose's emotions are clearly shown through her failure to see such a beautiful setting. In the later books, in particular, the outer world serves in almost every case as a reflection of the inner world which so fascinated Virginia. Clarissa's view of Bond Street, for example, in *Mrs Dalloway*, clearly reflects her own priorities in life — her deep respect for social order and her strong aesthetic sense. So that whilst being an external description, the following is also a description of Clarissa's inner world:

> Bond Street fascinated her; Bond Street early in the morning in the season; its flags flying; its shops; no splash; no glitter; one roll of tweed in the shop where her father had bought his suits for fifty years; a few pearls; salmon on an iceblock.
>
> 'That is all,' she said, looking at the fishmonger's. 'That is all,' she repeated, pausing for a moment at the window of a glove shop where, before the War, you could buy almost perfect gloves. And her old Uncle William used to say a lady is known by her shoes and her gloves. He had turned on his bed one morning in the middle of the War. He had said, 'I have had enough.' Gloves and shoes; she had a passion for gloves; but her own daughter, her Elizabeth, cared not a straw for either of them.
>
> Not a straw, she thought, going on up Bond Street to a shop where they kept flowers for her when she gave a party.

Septimus's view of Regent's Park, in the same novel, tells us something about the park, but, more importantly, shows us that though he, like Clarissa, loves Nature, he endows it with a terrifying life, indicative of his unstable state of mind:

He had only to open his eyes; but a weight was on them;
a fear. He strained; he pushed; he looked; he saw Regent's
Park before him. Long streamers of sunlight fawned at
his feet. The trees waved, brandished. We welcome, the
world seemed to say; we accept; we create. Beauty, the
world seemed to say. And as if to prove it (scientifically)
wherever he looked, at the houses, at the railings, at the
antelopes stretching over the palings, beauty sprang instantly. To watch a leaf quivering in the rush of air was
an exquisite joy. Up in the sky swallows swooping, swerv-
ing, flinging themselves in and out, round and round, yet
always with perfect control as if elastics held them; and
the flies rising and falling; and the sun spotting now this
leaf, now that, in mockery, dazzling it with soft gold
in pure good temper; and now and again some chime
(it might be a motor horn) tinkling divinely on the
grass stalks—all of this, calm and reasonable as it was,
made out of ordinary things as it was, was the truth
now; beauty, that was the truth now. Beauty was
everywhere. . . .

But the branches parted. A man in grey was actually
walking towards them. It was Evans!

As Katharine Hilbery in *Night and Day* waits for Ralph
Denham to emerge from his office in Lincoln's Inn
Fields her rapture is shown not so much by a direct
description of her mental state as by a physical description
of how she sees London at that moment:

The square itself, with its immense houses all so fully
occupied and stern of aspect, its atmosphere of industry
and power, as if even the sparrows and the children
were earning their daily bread, as if the sky itself, with
its grey and scarlet clouds, reflected the serious
intention of the city beneath it, spoke of him. Here
was the fit place for their meeting, she thought; here

was the fit place for her to walk thinking of him. She
could not help comparing it with the domestic streets
of Chelsea. With this comparison in her mind, she
extended her range a little, and turned into the main
road. The great torrent of vans and carts was sweep-
ing down Kingsway; pedestrians were streaming in two
currents along the pavements. She stood fascinated at
the corner. The deep roar filled her ears; the changing
tumult had the inexpressible fascination of varied
life pouring ceaselessly with a purpose which, as she
looked, seemed to her, somehow, the normal purpose
for which life was framed; its complete indifference
to the individuals, whom it swallowed up and rolled
onwards, filled her with at least a temporary exalt-
ation. The blend of daylight and of lamplight made
her an invisible spectator, just as it gave the people
who passed her a semi-transparent quality, and left
the faces pale ivory ovals in which the eyes alone
were dark. They tended the enormous rush of the
current—the great flow, the deep stream, the unquenchable tide. She stood unobserved and absorbed, glorying
openly in the rapture that had run subterraneously all
day.

Here the external scene is used skilfully to reflect
Katharine's feelings. She prefers to be in Lincoln's Inn
Fields rather than Chelsea because its bustle and purpose
entirely suits her mood. It is almost as though Virginia
had to take her to Lincoln's Inn Fields before she could
express her rapture.

As the inner world of Virginia's people is revealed to
us partly through setting, so too are their characters,
though Virginia did not intend us to think of them as
having 'character' in the Dickensian sense, particularly
in *The Waves*. In this, one of her most experimental
novels, Virginia sees her six actors playing out the Nine

Ages of man in terms of their adjustment to life, rather than of their inherent characteristics. Yet the reader does get a strong sense of 'character' in *The Waves* and one powerful way this is conveyed to us is through Susan's, Jinny's, Rhoda's, Louis', Neville's and Bernard's reactions to London, which they conveniently spell out for us. Susan and Jinny, who are in many ways opposites, have completely opposite reactions to the capital. Susan, the solid countrywoman, changing trains in London on her way home from boarding-school, vows:

> I will not send my children [away] to school nor spend a night all my life in London. Here in this vast station everything echoes and booms hollowly. The light is like the yellow light under an awning. Jinny lives here. Jinny takes her dog for walks on these pavements. People here shoot through the streets silently. They look at nothing but shop-windows. Their heads bob up and down all at the same height. The streets are laced together with telegraph wires. The houses are all glass, all festoons and glitter; now all front doors and lace curtains, all pillars and white steps. But now I pass on, out of London again; the fields begin again; and the houses, and women hanging washing, and trees and fields. London is now veiled, now vanished, now crumbled, now fallen.

Jinny, on the other hand, believes that Piccadilly tube station is 'where everything that is desirable meets — Piccadilly South Side, Piccadilly North Side, Regent Street and the Haymarket. I stand for a moment under the pavement in the heart of London. Innumerable wheels rush and feet press just over my head. The great avenues of civilization meet here and strike this way and that. I am in the heart of life.'

Louis, the poet, though succeeding in his highly

respectable job in a City bank, still lives in an attic room, whose view reflects his own somewhat bleak vision:

> Broken and soot-stained are these roofs with their chimney cowls, their loose slates, their slinking cats and attic windows. I pick my way over broken glass, among blistered tiles, and see only vile and famished faces.

Rhoda, a visionary like Louis, and like Virginia Woolf herself on whom she is almost certainly based, sees an even more sordid and horrifying London, particularly in its commercial centres:

> 'Oh, life, how I have dreaded you,' said Rhoda, 'oh, human beings, how I have hated you! How you have nudged, how you have interrupted, how hideous you have looked in Oxford Street, how squalid sitting opposite each other staring in the Tube!'

By contrast, Neville, who is also a writer, sees London in similar terms to Jinny. It seems to him the centre of civilization, a place that he hopes will provide him with the kind of amorous, sophisticated adventures he loves:

> The train slows and lengthens, as we approach London, the centre, and my heart draws out too, in fear, in exultation. I am about to meet—what? What extraordinary adventure waits me, among these mail vans, these porters, these swarms of people calling taxis. I feel insignificant, lost but exultant.

Finally Bernard, the spokesman for the six, responds to London with vivid imagination and ready phrases highly revealing of his character, which responds without judgement:

How fair, how strange, . . . glittering, many-pointed
and many-domed London lies before me under mist.
Guarded by gasometers, by factory chimneys, she lies
sleeping as we approach. She folds the ant-heap to her
breast. All cries, all clamour, are softly enveloped in
silence. Not Rome herself looks more majestic. But
we are aimed at her. Already her maternal somnolence
is uneasy. Ridges fledged with houses rise from the
mist. Factories, cathedrals, glass domes, institutions
and theatres erect themselves. The early train from
the north is hurled at her like a missile. We draw a
curtain as we pass. Blank expectant faces stare at us
as we rattle and flash through stations. Men clutch
their newspapers a little tighter, as our wind sweeps
them, envisaging death. But we roar on. We are about
to explode in the flanks of the city like a shell in the
side of some ponderous, maternal, majestic animal.
She hums and murmurs; she awaits us.

These are only a few examples of the way Virginia uses
her six voices' response to London to reveal more of
their character. Examples could equally well have been
taken from *Mrs Dalloway* or *The Years*. Such examples
would have been more difficult to find in earlier novels,
where London is more often used to reveal states of
mind rather than character.

An even more interesting, because more unusual, way
Virginia uses London is to help her shape her material,
to help give form to her novels. In discarding such 'outer',
shaping elements of fiction as elaborate plots and predict-
able characters and concentrating on the 'inner' stream
of consciousness, Virginia ran the risk of both incoherence
and shapelessness. Here London again comes to her aid.
The first clear example of this occurs in *Jacob's Room*.
In chapter thirteen, when Jacob has arrived back in
London from Greece the reader is led from Jacob himself

to each of the people who love him and in almost every case the apparently random material is shaped geographically by London. As Jacob sits in Hyde Park with his friend Bonamy, one of his admirers, Clara, sets out to walk in the same park with her dog and Mr Bowley, but does not meet Jacob. Meantime, Julia Eliot, though not meeting either Jacob or Clarissa as she also walks in Hyde Park, is nevertheless linked to Clarissa through *an incident they both notice — a runaway horse*. It is at the end of this scene that we are told the time:

> The watch on [Julia's] wrist gave her twelve minutes and a half in which to reach Bruton Street. Lady Congreve expected her at five.

The striking of five on a gilt clock in Regent Street is then used to link us to another of Jacob's admirers, Florinda, who is meeting Nick Bramham, but still thinking of Jacob. Yet a third admirer of Jacob, Fanny Elmer, is next shown walking aimlessly along the Strand thinking of him. The bus she catches to Piccadilly is held up in Whitehall by a procession which leads us to Jacob's other male friend, Timothy, the brother of Clara. It is at this point that Big Ben strikes five, so that we know that several of these scenes are meant to have taken place simultaneously. Jacob, who has been abandoned by Bonamy earlier on, now leaves Hyde Park by way of Piccadilly, where he is glimpsed by Clarissa, on her way from her house — 'in the square behind Sloane Street' — to Covent Garden Opera House. He is also seen by his old tutor, the Rev. Andrew Floyd. None of these characters talk to each other, yet their near-encounters give shape to what might otherwise seem entirely random.

Virginia herself, however, accepted the charge that her transitions in *Jacob's Room* were too jerky and in her next novel, *Mrs Dalloway*, made them far smoother and more formal. She achieved this mainly by bringing a particular stream of consciousness, whatever it may have been preoccupied with, to the present moment in time and place, by focussing upon some object, then caused another mind to focus upon the same object, thus moving to that mind, as she said, 'without spilling a drop'. In most cases the focus is provided by London. The two main strands of the plot (one connected with Clarissa, the other with Septimus) are linked by London scenes, though Clarissa and Septimus themselves never meet. By using more or less 'natural' scenes from the life of a big city, Virginia is able to make smoother, more flowing transitions between the two strands. This obviously appealed to her as less artificial, or more 'lifelike', than the elaborate plots full of coincidence and outer events of many nineteenth-century novels. If we look at some of the connections in *Mrs Dalloway*, they should show how crucial London is in the shaping process.

As the book opens Clarissa is going to Bond Street to buy flowers for her party that evening. Whilst choosing them she hears a car back-fire, a fairly commonplace experience in London in those days. The sound is also heard by Septimus, whose unstable mind interprets it ominously. He and his wife continue up Bond Street, through Harley Street, where they are to see an eminent psychiatrist, to wait for their appointment in Regent's Park. Once there Septimus notices a plane sky-writing something that he again interprets portentously. After several other people have tried to read the sky-writing it is seen by Clarissa, who is by now back at her Westminster home. This geographical link between Septimus and Clarissa is reinforced by Clarissa's old friend, Peter Walsh, who first visits her in Westminster, then walks by a slightly different route from the one she and Septimus have covered between them, to Regent's Park. As Peter sits musing over Clarissa in the park, a small child runs

full tilt into Septimus's wife, Rezia, who immediately
comforts her, and Peter's attention is drawn to
Septimus, again reinforcing the link. When Peter leaves
the park he gives a coin to an old beggar-woman singing
at Regent's Park tube. The same old woman is pitied by
Rezia as she follows shortly after with Septimus to keep
his appointment in Harley Street with Sir William Bradshaw. There are many other examples of such transitions,
most of which are scarcely noticeable on a first reading:
'Not a brick to be seen,' as Virginia hoped. The ambul-
ance bearing Septimus's mutilated body away after his
leap from his window is heard by Peter Walsh as he
returns to his hotel in Bloomsbury to change for
Clarissa's party, again linking Septimus tenuously to
Clarissa. Elizabeth Dalloway's bus ride to Fleet Street
from Westminster leads us back to Septimus lying on
his couch, by the perhaps over-ingenious device of yellow
sunshine and black shadows in Fleet Street turning into
black and yellow bananas in Septimus's fruit-bowl.
Another familiar feature of London life, Big Ben, is used
frequently both to link characters and to help the reader
place the various incidents in relation to each. As Richard
Dalloway enters Dean's Yard on his way home to give
Clarissa flowers, Big Ben is beginning to strike, a sound
which 'floods Clarissa's drawing-room, where she sat, ever
so annoyed, at her writing-table . . .' By the time Richard
has reached the house Big Ben has just finished striking
three, another landmark in the day, another clue to help
the reader follow the stream-of-consciousness without
drowning in it.

Virginia also shapes her material by repeating typical
London scenes, which seem to take on significance from
repetition. Near the beginning of *The Years*, Sir Digby
and Lady Pargiter are driving across the Serpentine with
their daughter Maggie:

There was the Serpentine, red in the *setting sun*; the
trees grouped together, sculptured, losing their detail;
and the ghostly architecture of the little *bridge*, *white*
at the end, *composed the scene*. The lights—the sunlight and the artificial light—were strangely mixed. . . .
   The cab passed over the bridge. *It entered the
shadow of the trees.* Now it left the Park and *joined
the long line of cabs*, taking *people in evening dress* to
plays, to dinner-parties, that was streaming towards
the Marble Arch. *The light* grew more and more
artificial; *yellower and yellower* . . . [my italics]

Years later in this chronicle novel Sir Digby's nephew,
Martin, having recently met his cousin Maggie in Kensington Gardens, crosses the same bridge in almost
identical words:

The *sun* was *setting* as he drove across the Park . . .
Now he was crossing the bridge over the Serpentine.
The water glowed with sunset light; twisted poles of
lamp light lay on the water, and there, at the end the
*white bridge composed the scene. The cab entered
the shadow of the trees*, and *joined the long line of
cabs* that was *streaming towards the Marble Arch.
People in evening dress* were going to *plays and parties.
The light* became *yellower and yellower.* [my italics]

The significance of the repetition of this typical London
scene is not easy to grasp, but Virginia may be trying to
explain when she causes Eleanor Pargiter to ask towards
the end of *The Years*: 'Does everything then come over
again a little differently? . . . If so, is there a pattern; a
theme, recurring like music; half remembered, half for-
gotten? . . . a gigantic pattern, momentarily perceptible?'
   Virginia rarely spells out her 'theme'. The reader has
usually to rely on his interpretation of scenes, events

134

and any other clues that are given. In some cases these
clues are given unobtrusively but firmly through the
background. In Virginia's day, even more than in our
own, social standing could generally be inferred from
the area of London inhabited. So that instead of spelling
out Clarissa's social privilege in *Mrs Dalloway*, Virginia
has only to mention her exquisite little house in Westminster for us to grasp the point. Similarly she has no
need to tell us of Septimus's humble social origins and
lack of social privilege, she has merely to refer to his
'lodgings off the Tottenham Court Road', in her day a
not very desirable area. In this particular instance it is
vital to her theme that we should possess these facts,
since we are faced with two main characters who are
shown to be very similar in some ways, yet end up very
differently. Both Septimus and Clarissa love Nature,
both are highly sensitive, perhaps over-sensitive, both
despair at times of contact with other people and suffer
from a strong sense of isolation. Of course, they can also
be seen as polar opposites. Clarissa may at times feel
isolation, but Septimus is at the negative pole of isolation.
Whereas Clarissa is able — and anxious — to relate to
others, as her parties clearly show, Septimus would
rather die than face a relatedness he can no longer believe
in. Whilst Clarissa finally recognises Septimus's individual
integrity as vital, however, she herself does not commit
suicide and the reader cannot help feeling that her personal and social situation has something to do with her
survival, though by no means all. She is to some extent
cushioned by her privileged existence, symbolized by
Westminster, whereas Septimus, in his Bloomsbury
lodging-house, is not. As I shall try to show in the next
chapter, Virginia's London has a well-defined symbolism,
which does not always coincide with our own.

Beside having a definite symbolic landscape, London
itself is a symbol for Virginia. It stands mainly for vitality

or life, that 'life' she was trying to put back into the novel, which she felt had become stale and conventional in the hands of writers like Arnold Bennett, H.G. Wells and John Galsworthy. London was, in Virginia's own words, 'life to [her]' and she rarely failed to respond to it. In London she feels she is 'on the higher crest of the biggest wave—right in the centre and swim of things'. Looking back in 1933 over nearly ten years in central London after leaving Richmond, Virginia writes: 'Well we are very happy. Life buds and sprouts all around us'. From her second novel onwards Virginia uses London as a symbol of life and vitality. Clarissa in *Mrs Dalloway* equates 'London' with 'life' as she waits to cross Victoria Street on a lovely summer's day. Jinny, Neville and Bernard in *The Waves* and Mary Datchet in *Night and Day*, all regard London as the centre of the universe and are stimulated almost excessively by it. Eleanor Pargiter of *The Years* perfectly reflects Virginia's own feelings as she sits in a London bus: 'She relaxed; she breathed in the soft London air; she heard the dull London roar with pleasure. She looked along the street and relished the sight of cabs, vans and carriages all trotting past with an end in view. She liked coming back in October to the full stir of life after the summer was over.'

Eleanor, like Virginia, finds London exciting partly because of its bustle. Virginia loves its strong sense of history, which adds greatly to its vitality for her. Reviewing *London Revisited* by E.V. Lucas, she writes:

> From the bones of extinct monsters and the coins of Roman emperors in the cellars to the name of the shopman over the door, the whole story is fascinating and the material endless. Perhaps Cockneys are a prejudiced race, but certainly this inexhaustible richness seems to belong to London more than to any other great city.

Reading Defoe, Virginia has no problem seeing London
as it looked in the early eighteenth century: 'I saw
London, in particular the view of white city churches
and palaces from Hungerford Bridge through the eyes
of Defoe. I saw the old women selling matches through
his eyes; and the draggled girl skirting round the pavement of St James's Square seemed to me out of Roxana
or Moll Flanders.' Virginia is particularly fond of the
eighteenth century. She imagines mail-coaches 'running
into London in the eighteenth century' in *Jacob's Room*.
In the same novel the architecture of Lamb's Conduit
Street arouses her historic sense:

> Long ago great people lived here, and coming back
> from Court, past midnight stood, huddling their satin
> skirts, under the carved door-posts while the footman
> roused himself from his mattress on the floor, hurried-
> ly fastened the lower buttons of his waistcoat, and let
> them in. The bitter eighteenth century rain rushed
> down the kennel.

Both this and another, recurring passage, on the 'distinct-
ion' of the eighteenth-century panelling and carving in
Jacob's Room, reinforce Virginia's attempt to convey
Jacob's own 'distinction'. ('So distinguished-looking'
Mrs Durrant remarks, in an attempt to sum him up.)
Virginia is not merely indulging her love of London's
history in her novels, she is using it in various ways to
forward her ideas. When describing William Rodney's
rooms in a small court of eighteenth-century houses off
Fleet Street, for example, she invokes the shade of Dr
Johnson to recreate the antiquity and mysteriousness
of the scene and perhaps also the relative insignificance
of William Rodney and the problems he is later to face.
For Virginia is constantly aware of the smallness of
human beings in the whole time-scale of history. Her

beggar-woman singing at Regent's Park tube station in
Mrs Dalloway makes us feel for a moment, the brief and
trivial nature of our own lives, and even those of Peter
Walsh and Septimus, who hear her:

> Through all ages — when the pavement was grass, when
> it was swamp, through the age of tusk and mammoth,
> through the age of silent sunrise — the battered woman
> — for she wore a skirt — with her right hand exposed,
> her left clutching at her side, stood singing of love —
> love which has lasted a million years, she sang, love
> which prevails, and millions of years ago her lover,
> who had been dead these centuries, had walked, she
> crooned, with her in May; . . .
>
> As the ancient song bubbled up opposite Regent's
> Park Tube Station, still the earth seemed green and
> flowery; still, though it issued from so rude a mouth,
> a mere hole in the earth, muddy too, matted with
> root fibres and tangled grasses, still the old bubbling
> burbling song, soaking through the knotted roots of
> infinite ages, and skeletons and treasure, streamed
> away in rivulets over the pavement and all along the
> Marylebone Road, and down towards Euston, fertiliz-
> ing, leaving a damp stain.

Virginia's own powerful sense of prehistoric London is
shared by several of her characters and in each case
indicates a person of vivid imagination and some wisdom.
Bernard, Virginia's spokesman in *The Waves*, cannot
tread the streets of London without instantly recalling
its long past:

> People might walk through me . . . The growl of the
> traffic might be any uproar — forest trees or the roar
> of wild beasts . . . Beneath these pavements are shells,
> bones and silence.

Virginia's most obvious use of London's history occurs
in *Orlando*, where her detailed descriptions of the changing background convey obliquely but vividly the passing
of time. Orlando herself (for she has now become a
woman) measures her long absence from England by the
changes which have occurred in London. Since her last
visit in the seventeenth century, when she (then a man)
visited the Royal Pavilion on the ice at Greenwich,
London's skyline has altered out of all recognition, under-
lining the length of her absence:

> 'St Paul's,' said Captain Bartolus, who stood by her
> side [as their ship sails up the Thames], 'The Tower
> of London,' he continued. 'Greenwich Hospital, erect-
> ed in memory of Queen Mary by her husband, his late
> Majesty, William the Third. Westminster Abbey. The
> Houses of Parliament.' As he spoke, each of these
> famous buildings rose to view. It was a fine September
> morning. A myriad of little water-craft plied from
> bank to bank. Rarely has a gayer, or more interesting,
> spectacle presented itself to the gaze of a returned
> traveller. Orlando hung over the prow. Her eyes had
> been used too long to savages and nature not to be
> entranced by these urban glories. That, then, was the
> dome of St Paul's which Mr Wren had built during her
> absence. Near by, a shock of golden hair burst from a
> pillar — Captain Bartolus was at her side to inform her
> that that was the Monument; there had been a plague
> and a fire during her absence. . . . Here, she thought,
> had been the great carnival. Here, where the waves
> slapped briskly, had stood the Royal Pavilion.

Other changes are emphasized through setting: the 'seven-
teenth-century huddle of little black, beetle-browed
houses' and cobbled pavements have given way to 'broad
and orderly thoroughfares' and dignified eighteenth-

century houses. In order finally to catch the spirit of the age Virginia has Captain Bartolus point out Addison, Dryden and Pope (impossible as she knows it is that these should be together) in the coffee-houses that have replaced the Elizabethan taverns for the literati. When Orlando reaches the nineteenth century, the coffee-houses have been replaced by restaurants and the streets of London have become louder, more crowded and, symbolically, much darker. By the twentieth century London seems to have shrunk and, at the same time, to have become lighter after the passing of Victorianism. The passage of the centuries has been completed and mainly by the simple but subtle device of describing London's architectural history.

Virginia's London is charged not only with history but also with great emotion. She finds poetic, even mystical significance in many of its scenes. There was, for her, 'something central and inexplicable', in even its most apparently mundane sights. While living in exile in Richmond she would become wildly excited when allowed a day in London, as this extract from her 1918 diary shows:

> I went to London on my usual round; the one I like best [i.e. Partridge and Cooper's stationery shop in Fleet Street, Gordon Square, Mudie's Lending Library in New Oxford Street and the 17 Club in Soho]. In my beatific state I forgot the principal thing I'd gone for; a typewriter ribbon; but never mind; that will be another day's treat.

She was 'filled with joy' in November 1923 when she thought she was going to move from Richmond to Woburn Square, and this joy both spilled over into and was caused by a trip to Waterloo Road, not conventionally thought of as a magical place:

> . . . it was so lovely in the Waterloo Road that it
> struck me that we were writing Shakespeare; by which
> I mean that when live people, seeming happy, produce
> an effect of beauty, and you don't have it offered as a
> work of art, but it seems a natural gift of theirs, then
> . . . somehow it affected me as I am affected by read-
> ing Shakespeare. No: it's life; going on in these very
> beautiful surroundings.

Walking through Russell Square on a cloudy but moonlit
night Virginia feels that she has almost had the great
revelation about life she longs for: 'I have a great and
astonishing sense of something there which is "it"—it is
not exactly beauty that I mean. It is that the thing is in
itself enough; satisfactory; achieved.' Such mystical states,
she was convinced, depended on 'having been in the stir
of London for some time'. The beauty Virginia sees in
London is not the conventional beauty of the sight-seeing
tour, as her reference to Waterloo Road shows. In fact,
it is often found in surprising places.

Virginia makes frequent use of her mystical vision of
London in her novels, to express that 'something central'
which may be 'inexplicable' but which she nevertheless
wants to convey. The beggarwoman singing at Regent's
Park tube in *Mrs Dalloway* is one example of this. There
is another even more convincing example in *Jacob's
Room*. Again the scene contains a vagrant, singing in the
streets of London:

> Long past sunset an old blind woman sat on a camp-
> stool with her back on the stone-wall of the Union
> of London and Smith's Bank, clasping a brown mongrel
> tight in her arms and singing out loud, not for coppers,
> no, from the depths of her wild gay heart—her sinful,
> tanned heart—for the child who fetches her is the fruit
> of sin, and should have been in bed, curtained, asleep,

instead of hearing in the lamplight her mother's wild
song, where she sits against the Bank, singing not for
coppers, with her dog against her breast.

Home they went. The grey church spires received
them; the hoary city, old, sinful, and majestic. One
behind another, round or pointed, piercing the sky or
massing themselves, like sailing ships, like granite cliffs,
spires and offices, wharves and factories crowd the
bank; eternally the pilgrims trudge; barges rest in mid
stream heavy laden; as some believe, the city loves her
prostitutes.

If we are in any doubt as to Virginia's meaning in this
common London scene, we have her diary account of
the actual incident which gave rise to the fictional scene
and a full explanation of its strange significance for her:

An old beggar woman, blind, sat against a stone wall
in Kingsway, holding a brown mongrel in her arms
and sang aloud. There was a recklessness about her;
much in the spirit of London. Defiant—almost gay,
clasping her dog as if for warmth. How many Junes
has she sat there, in the heart of London? How she
came to be there, what scenes she can go through, I
can't imagine. O damn it all, I say, why can't I know
all that too? Perhaps it was the song at night that seemed strange; she was singing shrilly, but for her own
amusement; not begging. Then the fire engines came by
—shrill too; with their helmets pale yellow in the moonlight. Sometimes everything gets into the same mood;
how to define this one I don't know—it was gay, and yet
terrible and fearfully vivid. Nowadays I'm often over-
come by London; even think of the dead who have walked in the city. Perhaps one might visit the churches. The
view of the grey white spires from Hungerford Bridge
brings it to me; and yet I can't say what 'it' is.

This example is particularly interesting because it shows how Virginia takes an incident from real life, records it in her diary and then uses it, with some of the same phrases, in her fiction. It also helps us to understand Virginia's very real appreciation of London in all its aspects and its central role in her work.

3

Symbolic Landscape

But each Londoner has a London in his mind which
is the real London, some denying the right of Bays-
water to be included, others of Kensington, and each
feels for London as he feels for his family, quietly but
deeply, and with a quick eye for affront.

Virginia Woolf's London is a very personal one. In keeping with her intense vision of the capital, it is also
frequently symbolic, the symbolism springing mainly
from her personal experience. Kensington and Chelsea,
for instance, stand for social respectability, Bloomsbury
for Bohemianism. Fleet Street and the City represent the
world of business, which Elizabeth Dalloway contrasts
longingly with her mother's Westminster world of social-
izing and parties. London parks and squares have each
their particular shade of emotion and London landmarks,
such as Big Ben, St Paul's and Westminster Abbey are seen
in almost wholly personal terms. Virginia's London is as
distinctive as that of Dickens, Pepys or Johnson and
claims our attention, both for its own sake and for the
light it throws on her work. It creates a kind of short-hand
which enriches our reading of her novels.

Those who know London well may feel that its symbolism is all too obvious, even allowing for the personality
of the writer describing it. London has, however, changed
a great deal since Virginia's day and so, accordingly, has
its symbolism. Chelsea, for example, is today regarded
as the home of both the wealthy and the Bohemian, whereas Virginia saw it largely as a place inhabited by her rich
or aristocratic friends. There has been an increasing
blurring of the edges and a far greater social mobility in
London, so that it is now possible, even desirable to live

145

in previously 'slummy' areas such as Lambeth, Dalston or Kentish Town. From being a clearly defined three-class society with each district sharply delineated, London has become much more of a two-class society, whose rich continue to live in Belgravia and Mayfair and whose 'others' can live virtually anywhere they choose.

It is quite clear that Virginia, living before such changes, divided London mentally into three — the centre, the suburbs and the slums. Of these she certainly preferred central London. When she returned to Bloomsbury from Richmond in 1924, she felt like a prisoner coming home from exile, though she had appreciated Richmond in its own way. Just as she adored central London for its vitality, so she preferred the slums to the suburbs, theoretically at least, because they seemed to her more alive. There is a revealing scene in *Jacob's Room* where Jacob, lunching with Lady Rocksbier in Mayfair, sees Moll Pratt from the slums and Mrs Hilda Thomas from the suburbs:

> The Countess of Rocksbier sat at the head of the table alone with Jacob. . . . Behind her (the window looked on Grosvenor Square) stood Moll Pratt on the pavement, offering violets for sale; and Mrs Hilda Thomas, lifting her skirts, preparing to cross the road. One was from Walworth; the other from Putney. Both wore black stockings, but Mrs Thomas was coiled in furs. The comparison was much in Lady Rocksbier's favour. Moll had more humour, but was violent; stupid too. Hilda Thomas was mealy-mouthed, all her silver frames aslant; egg-cups in the drawing-room; and the windows shrouded. Lady Rocksbier, whatever the deficiencies of her profile, had been a great rider to hounds. She used her knife with authority, tore her chicken bones, asking Jacob's pardon, with her own hands.

The superiority of the inhabitants of central London over both the slums and the suburbs is quite clear here and there is more than a touch of snobbishness in the judgement. Because London has changed so much since Virginia's day, it is now necessary to explore what she meant by these divisions and how she saw each area, starting with central London.

Central London

Apart from her forced retirement to Richmond, Virginia spent most of her adult life in central London and feels very much as Mary Datchett does in *Night and Day* about 'the wonderful maze of London, which still seemed to her . . . like a vast electric light, casting radiance upon the myriads of men and women who crowded round it. And here she was at the very centre of it all . . .' The centre for Virginia was undoubtedly Bloomsbury.

Bloomsbury

For most people Bloomsbury has become associated with artists and intellectuals, but it is important to remember that Virginia and her friends were partly responsible for these connotations. Obviously an area which contains London University, the British Museum and the Slade School of Art tends to attract artists and intellectuals, which was doubtless one reason Virginia's sister, Vanessa, chose to move from Kensington to Bloomsbury when their father died. Once there, however, she and Virginia formed the centre of a circle which lent both weight and respectability to what had previously been seen as a slightly disreputable district. For Virginia the centre of her group of friends always remained her first Bloomsbury

home, Gordon Square. Long after she had left number
46 she felt it to be her personal centre of the universe.
Returning to Richmond from a party there one dark January night she tried to explain to herself why she loved
it so:

> Suppose one's normal pulse to be 70: in five minutes it
> was 120: and the blood, not the sticky whitish fluid of
> daytime, but brilliant and prickling like champagne . . .
> There is something indescribably congenial to me in
> this easy artists' talk; the values the same as my own
> and therefore right; no impediments; life charming;
> good and interesting; no effort; art brooding calmly
> over it all; and none of this attachment to mundane
> things which I find in Chelsea.

In other moods Virginia felt threatened by Gordon Square
society, which included at various phases Maynard Keynes,
Lytton Strachey, Vanessa Bell, Clive Bell and his long-
standing mistress, Mary Hutchinson, Adrian Stephen,
James Strachey and Ralph Partridge. Faced with such a
challenging group, Virginia felt at times as though she
were in the lions' house at the zoo: 'One goes from cage
to cage. All the animals are dangerous, rather suspicious
of each other, and full of fascination and mystery.' On the
whole, however, she felt stimulated and liberated by her
friends in Gordon Square. Leonard initially feared their
effect on her, following her breakdown, and it was only
after nine years' rest in Richmond that he reluctantly allowed her to return to the neighbourhood. Virginia chose a
house in Tavistock Square, partly because of its nearness
to Gordon Square, partly because she loved London
squares. Before her breakdown she had enjoyed living in
Gordon, Fitzroy and Brunswick Squares. 'Bloomsbury
squares always intoxicate me with their beauty,' she wrote
a month after her return in February 1924 to Lady

Ottoline Morrell, who had just moved into the nearby
Bedford Square. In these 'tree-sprinkled, grass-grown
spaces' Virginia could imagine herself in the country,
particularly at night. One of her favourite occupations in
early summer was what she called 'street sauntering and
square haunting'.

In contrast to the squares with their orderly houses,
neat iron railings, trees, grass and flowers, Virginia also
loved Holborn's 'dusky' streets. The 'tumult and riot and
busyness [sic] of it all' stirred her imagination in a quite
different way from the peaceful squares. Crowded streets
were the only places, she believed, that ever made her
'what-in-the-case of another-[you]-might-call think'.
Jacob Flanders in *Jacob's Room*, who lives in or near
Lamb's Conduit Street, finds human life is very tolerable
on the top of an omnibus in Holborn. Virginia herself
feels curiously free as she reaches Holborn on a bus bringing her from Park Lane, which seems to her socially suffocating.

The City

Holborn was close to Leonard's office at *The Nation* in
Great James Street which runs north off Theobald's
Road, near the junction with Gray's Inn Road. Whilst
still exiled in Richmond Virginia dreamt of starting off
early one day at Leonard's office and walking through the
City streets to Wapping. For she loved the City almost as
much as Bloomsbury and had her favourite walks there
(see pages 189-93). As late as 1938 she calls herself rather
proudly, 'shabby, city haunting Virginia'. When she and
Leonard were first married and looking for a place of their
own in 1912, they chose rooms in Clifford's Inn, just off
Fleet Street. Not only did the City symbolize the business
world for Virginia, it also seemed to her a place of

mystery and excitement. She enjoyed losing herself in the maze of little half-lit streets round the old Printing House Square near Blackfriars Bridge. Her usual round when up from Richmond for a precious day in London would start at Partridge and Cooper, a large stationers on the corner of Fleet Street and Chancery Lane, and continue with a walk through Lincoln's Inn Fields to Mudie's Lending Library in New Oxford Street. From there it was a short step to Gordon Square, a walk she had often taken from her Clifford's Inn flat to visit Vanessa and other friends. Virginia frequently mentions the Strand in her novels; it is not the well-known part of it she means, but the end which runs from Aldwych past the Law Courts to the Temple. Like Terence Hewet, who reminisces about this area in *The Voyage Out*, she must often have walked along this eastern section of the Strand and turned into the seclusion of the Inns of Court at the Temple to escape the uproar. This end of the Strand generally signifies for Virginia a place for serious thought, rather than intense emotion. Katharine Hilbery realises this in *Night and Day* when she goes there to try to understand her relations with William Rodney.

Kensington

Of all the places Virginia inhabited, she least liked Kensington. Associating it as she did with the social respectability of her youth, she found it, in retrospect at least, suffocating. South Kensington she found even more oppressive, because even more dedicated to 'being on the safe side and doing the thing handsomely'. She was to some extent fascinated and certainly disarmed by what she called 'mounds of South Kensington dowager respectability'. Yet every time she succumbed to an invitation from Bruce Richmond, the editor of *The Times Literary*

Supplement, who lived at 23 Cromwell House, opposite
the Natural History Museum, she regretted it. Whilst she
admired the kindness and consideration she found there—
'Another cup of tea? Do for goodness sake take this armchair—and let me fetch you a slice of bread and butter'—
she disliked their blandness. Not only did the company
lack 'bite', they were also 'dowdy', her favourite word for
Kensington. Worst of all Kensington reminded her of her
step-brothers, George and Gerald Duckworth, and her
cousins 'Marny' and Emma Vaughan, whom she found as
unsavoury as the smell of cooked cabbage. However, not
all her memories of Kensington were unpleasant and years
later she still enjoyed walking in Kensington Gardens as
she had as a child.

The West End

Virginia felt almost as ambivalent about the West End as
she did about Kensington. By 'West End' she seems to
have meant Mayfair, Belgravia, Knightsbridge, Piccadilly
and parts of Victoria. At times it filled her with aversion,
particularly when she saw 'fat grandees' sitting in their
cars 'like portly jewels in satin cases'. Unlike Clarissa
Dalloway, she could feel paralysed by Bond Street, particularly when she had to buy clothes there. On other
occasions she admired the smartness and gaiety of the
West End, especially in the season when 'flags flew; canes
tapped; dresses flowed; and houses freshly painted had
awnings spread and swinging baskets of real geraniums'.
Like Mrs Dalloway, something in Virginia is stirred by the
discrete wealth and privilege of Belgravia and Mayfair.
She herself had tried to rent a house in Barton Street in
1923, perhaps the same one she places the Dalloways in,
but had found it too expensive. On that occasion she had
written in her diary: 'Westminster, noiseless and shadow-

ed, by the Abbey, is almost the heart of London'.

We can reasonably infer from the description of Jacob's visit to Lady Rocksbier in Grosvenor Square that Virginia was intrigued by the aristocracy and this extended to the areas they inhabited. Her attitude to a family friend, Lady 'Nelly' Cecil, who also lived in Grosvenor Square, reveals a deep respect, a fascination and, at the same time, a faint condescension which stemmed from a sense of intellectual superiority. Yet for all their apparent superficiality Virginia found the aristocracy far less dreary than Kensington society and this emerges symbolically in her description of Mayfair. It positively sparkles with life in the following passage taken from *The Years*:

> Although it was close on midnight, it scarcely seemed
> to be night; but rather some ethereal disembodied day,
> for there were so many lamps in the streets; cars passing;
> men in white mufflers with their light overcoats open
> walking along the clean dry pavements, and many
> houses were still lit up, for everyone was giving parties.

Lacking the social distinction of Mayfair and Belgravia, other areas of the West End are on the whole antipathetic to to Virginia. Piccadilly, for instance, is attractive to the character in *The Waves* whom Virginia portrays as somewhat superficial, Jinny (see page 128). Virginia's own attitude is often much closer to Jinny's moment of panic when she sees her ageing body in a mirror near Piccadilly tube: the crowds descending the escalator seem to her like 'the pinioned and terrible descent of some army of the dead down the moving stairs'. In the same novel, Rhoda, who most nearly resembles Virginia, feels panic in Oxford Street precisely because of its centrality and popularity. Amongst such crowds she loses all sense of meaning or purpose, seeing only 'hate, jealousy, hurry and indifference froth[ing] into the wild semblance of life' (see page 129). This is not Virginia's only view of Oxford Street. In a series of five essays about London commissioned by *Ideal Home* magazine, she devotes an entire piece to Oxford Street. Starting with the premise that it is *not* London's most distinguished thoroughfare, she goes on to defend the garishness and gaudiness of the street on other grounds: 'It is like the pebbly bed of a river whose stones are for ever washed by a bright stream. Everything glitters and twinkles'. Nevertheless, it is quite clear that Oxford Street is not one of Virginia's favourite haunts.

Charing Cross Road, on the other hand, though almost as busy, attracts her far more. For one thing it was not as frantic nor as commercial as Oxford Street in her day and what commerce there was centred round books — 'a paradise of bookshops', Virginia called it. Whilst rummaging for her own bargains she often bumped into Roger Fry in his wide-awake hat, clutching four or five yellow French books under his arm. Another reason she loved Charing Cross Road was that it led to Gerrard Street, where she and her friends had started the Seventeen Club in 1917, ostensibly to provide a meeting place for people interested in peace and democracy. In reality it turned out to be another useful meeting point for the group and, as such, figured in Virginia's usual London round when up from Richmond. Almost every member of the group went for tea there some time during the week. Virginia loved turning into the Seventeen Club and finding, or expecting to find someone she wanted to talk to. Nearby there was the added attraction of such Soho street-markets as Berwick and Rupert Streets. Virginia, who loved bargains, came away from them on one occasion with six bundles of coloured tapers she could not resist. Quite apart from the cheapness of these Soho markets, she loved their stir and colour, which often caused her to make a detour to visit them. The noise and crowds helped rouse in her the visions needed for her books.

Chelsea

At the edge of central London, just beyond Knightsbridge, yet not quite a suburb, lay Chelsea. About Chelsea Virginia had strong views. Fashionable as it was, Chelsea also had intellectual aspirations, unlike Mayfair. This provoked a sense of rivalry in Virginia, which focussed itself primarily on the unfortunate Logan Pearsall Smith. Essayist and bibliophile, Logan had come over from America to settle in England and, like many Americans, chose to live in Chelsea. Virginia seems to have regarded not only Logan, but most other members of the Chelsea intelligentsia as both dilettante and materialistic. Certainly they were wealthier on the whole than the Bloomsberries. They also prided themselves on, or cared more for, their social standing. When Virginia was not accusing them of 'attachment to mundane things', she was objecting to their 'mix up of letters and coronets', yet as she also confessed there were a good many coronets in Bloomsbury by the mid 1930s.

One of Chelsea's 'coronets' was in fact Virginia's own relative, Lady Ritchie, who had moved to St Leonard's Terrace from St George's Square after her husband's death in 1912. Logan Pearsall Smith lived at number 11 in the same street and at number 21 lived a friend of Logan's James Whittall, who longed to work for the Hogarth Press. It is quite possible that he was rejected merely because of his address, for Virginia admitted that she was 'a little alarmed at the social values of Mr W. for we don't want the Press to be a fashionable hobby patronised and inspired by Chelsea'. It is quite clear that she suffered her usual fascination with the 'hostesses' of Chelsea. Time and again she accepted invitations to Lady Sybil Colefax's grand evening parties at Argyll House in the King's Road, and to Ethel Sands' no less lavish evenings at 15 The Vale. She dined with the Sitwells several times when they lived at 2 Carlyle Square, though in their case she was less critical, since they did seem to her genuine artists. By 1930 she had resolved never to dine with Lady Colefax again, though she never quite managed to keep her resolution. In Virginia's novels Chelsea quite unequivocally stands for social privilege as opposed to intellect. The symbolism of *Night and Day* centres round the contrast between Katharine Hilbery's socially privileged but intellectually arid home in Cheyne Walk, Chelsea, and Ralph Denham's socially inferior but intellectually lively house in the suburbs at Highgate. Katharine's decision to marry Ralph involves leaving her Chelsea home. In doing so she frees herself to pursue her own intellectual interests, which are not understood by her family.

The Suburbs

The placing of Ralph Denham's family in the suburbs is significant. Not only does it allude to Leonard Woolf's own family home at Putney, on which it is clearly based, it also reveals Virginia's deep suspicion of the suburbs. When she and Leonard were choosing a quiet place to live in 1914, during a lull in her breakdown, they rejected both Highgate and Hampstead and chose Richmond because they considered it to be not an offshoot of London, but a town in its own right.

Richmond

It is clear that Virginia appreciated Richmond while she was in need of rest. She could walk in Richmond Park,

Kew Gardens or by the river. On days off she and Leonard could visit Ham House, or wander round Hampton Court

Hampton Court

When Ralph, Katharine, William and Cassandra finally resolve their emotional tangle in *Night and Day* they celebrate with a trip to Hampton Court. For Rhoda in *The Waves*, who loses all sense of meaning in Oxford Street, Hampton Court also symbolizes order and sanity: ' . . . shall I go to Hampton Court and look at the red walls and courtyards and the seemliness of herded yew trees making black pyramids symmetrically on the grass among the flowers? There shall I recover beauty and impose order upon my raked, my dishevelled soul?' It is clearly Virginia who speaks. When the six characters of *The Waves* meet in middle age Hampton Court is chosen, partly because of its sense of history and, therefore, of time, which has begun to preoccupy several of them.

Greenwich

Greenwich plays a similar role to Hampton Court both in Virginia's life and her works. On at least one occasion in her her diary she records how she decides to deal with a particularly aimless state with a visit to Greenwich. Rhoda in *The Waves* almost certainly echoes Virginia's reactions on arriving at this historic place, one of whose attractions is its nearness to the Thames and the docks:

> Now from the window of the tram I see masts among chimneys; there is the river; there are ships that sail to India. I will walk by the river. I will pace this embankment, where an old man reads a newspaper in a glass

shelter. I will pace this terrace and watch the ships bowling down the tide. . . . Now I will relinquish; now I will let loose. Now I will at last free the jerked-back desire to be spent, to be consumed.

Greenwich also features prominently in *Orlando* as the home of the English Court during the Great Frost of the early seventeenth century, when Orlando meets his Russian Princess in scenes of great gaiety. There is the same idea of orderliness attached to Greenwich as to Hampton Court. In both cases it seems to stem from their strong sense of history.

Highgate

Suburbs nearer to the centre of London have less appeal for Virginia, possibly because she is less aware of their history. Apart from her description of Highgate in *Night and Day*, with its 'suburban streets and damp shrubs growing in front gardens and the absurd names painted in white upon the gates of those gardens,' she has little to say about it.

Putney

Putney, where Virginia visited Leonard's mother in Colinette Road, clearly depressed her even more. Even Leonard, who had lived there on and off for twenty years, felt oppressed by it on his return from Ceylon. But it was Virginia's visit to Leonard's brother and his wife, Edgar and Sylvia, at 7 Castello Avenue, which provoked her fiercest attack on the suburbs:

The streets of villas make me more dismal than slums.

Each has a cropped-tree growing out of a square lifted from the pavement in front of it. Then the interiors — But I don't want to dwell on this. As Leonard said, it's the soul of Sylvia in stucco.

Leonard and Virginia may have chosen to live in Richmond in 1914 partly because it was near his mother. It certainly did not encourage Virginia to visit 'Lady', as she was called, and Leonard usually went alone.

Hampstead

It is clearly the lack of vitality which irritated Virginia in Putney. In Hampstead it was the high-mindedness and smugness; 'the immaculate and moral heights of Hampstead' she dubbed it. As with Chelsea, she felt threatened by Hampstead, regarding it as the enemy's camp. Her usual method of dealing with enemies was satire and it is not lacking here. When in 1914 she felt obliged to attend a Union of Democratic Control meeting which Leonard was addressing, she could not resist a dig at the audience: 'such clean, decorous, un-compromising and high-minded old ladies and old gentlemen; and the young wearing brown clothes, and thinking seriously, the women dowdy, the men narrow-shouldered; bright fire and lights and books surrounding us, and everyone of course agreeing beforehand to what was said.' Hampstead, she felt, was too full of 'types'. Explaining her objection to John Middleton Murry's friend, John Sullivan, she protested 'Sullivan is too much of the india-rubber faced, mobile-lipped, unshaven, uncombed, black, uncompromising, suspicious, powerful man of genius in Hampstead type for my taste'. She had great fun sending up Edward Garnett's mistress, Nellie Heath: 'the top half Esquimaux, the bottom Maytime in Hampstead — sprigged muslin, sandals'. Even her old friend and tutor, Janet Case, was not immune. Returning

from a visit to Janet and her sister Emphie in 1916 she
wrote to Vanessa:

Janet is still more or less bedridden, and keeps her disease
in the dark, though she was writing an article upon illegit-
imacy in Sweden for a newspaper. Downstairs, Emphie
was playing very badly on the violin to a party of wounded
soldiers. The house is crowded with photographs of old
pupils, deceased parents and the Elgin Marbles, and they
have covers to all the po's. Does this convey any of the
spirit of Hampstead to you?

Virginia was even less merciful towards the editor of the
New Statesman, Kingsley Martin and his wife who lived, she
told Ethel Smyth, 'in a high airy brainy room at Hampstead,
where there's nuts on a check tablecloth and autotypes from
Albert Durer [*sic*] on a mud coloured wall'.

Even though she did not admire Hampstead, Virginia was
impressed by its distinctiveness. In an article written for
Ideal Home in the early 1930s, she stressed that Hampstead
had always remained a place with a character peculiar to itself. She loved walking on the Heath, particularly at Parliament Hill, where she could look down on London 'crowded
and ribbed and compact'. Apart from these walks she also
enjoyed visiting Kenwood House and Keats' House in Keats'
Grove, where she vividly imagines him at his window reading
and writing. Most of all perhaps she liked Hampstead for the
friends she and Leonard visited there, particularly during the
Richmond period. Whilst Leonard consulted with Margaret
Llewellyn Davies, the General Secretary of the Women's Co-
operative Guild, at her house at 28 Church Row, later 26
Well Walk, Virginia would go to see Janet Case at 5 Windmill
Hill. Virginia also took to visiting Katherine Mansfield in
1918, when the New Zealand writer was living with John
Middleton Murry at 2 Portland Villas, East Heath Road —
the 'Elephant' as the squat little house was called. For a time

Virginia attended Dorothy Brett's Thursday evenings at
6 Pond Street. 'Brett', as this titled lady was called, was a
friend, or rather a disciple, of D.H. Lawrence, whom she
eventually followed to America, where Vita Sackville-
West visited her many years later. At Brett's 'evenings'
Virginia might meet the Middleton Murrys, the 'man of
genius in Hampstead' John Sullivan, Sydney Waterlow or
Koteliansky, a Russian *émigré* who translated several
books for the Hogarth Press. On the whole Virginia found
the company 'unsympathetic', her main criticism of
Hampstead society.

The Slums

Virginia may not have liked the suburbs on the whole,
but at least she knew them. About the slums, though
theoretically preferring them, she is less convincing. Her
only real contact with them occurred between 1905 and
1907 when she taught at the Working Men's College in
Waterloo Road which has since become Morley College.
This is probably one reason she tends to place her poor
south of the river. Her rather condescending attitude towards them, even when she appears to be praising their
vitality, emerges very clearly in a passage from *Jacob's
Room*:

> It seems as if the poor had gone raiding the town, and
> now trapesed back to their own quarters, like beetles
> scurrying to their holes, for that old woman fairly
> hobbles towards Waterloo, grasping a shiny bag, as if
> she had been out into the light and now made off with
> some scraped chicken bones to her hovel underground.
> On the other hand, though the wind is rough and blow-
> ing in their faces, those girls there, striding hand in
> hand, shouting out a song, seem to feel neither cold

nor shame. They are hatless. They triumph.

Lambeth

Lambeth was undoubtedly a slum in Virginia's day, so that when Sally Pargiter goes to live there after her parents die in *The Years*, she is definitely showing her lack of concern for social values. She is also helping to reinforce Virginia's point about the vitality of the slums. As a dreamer, perhaps even a visionary, Sally sees only the essentials, Virginia seems to suggest, so that she is not depressed by the sordidness of her surroundings. Her cousin Rose, visiting her in Hyams Place, is more sensitive to the social nuances and less impressed by its vitality. After her sister marries, Sally moves to equally slummy lodgings in Milton Street near the Tower of London. This time it is her cousin, North Pargiter, who visits her. His reaction is even more direct than Rose's: 'What a dirty, sordid, low-down street to live in'. Yet he is fascinated by Sally's choice and wants to know why she always chooses slums. The reader is left to deduce the answer from Sally's unworldliness and mysticism. Virginia does not attempt to describe Sally's second lodgings, presumably because she was not sufficiently sure of the details. She does, however, describe the fringes of Clerkenwell, which she knew fairly well from her visits to Leonard's office at Great James Street and her walks in the City. As Virginia passed Red Lion Square, just off Theobald's Road, she probably felt as Eleanor Pargiter did when she visited her sister Delia there. The passage emphasizes just how much London has changed since Virginia's day:

> The streets they were driving through were horribly poor; and not only poor, she thought, but vicious. Here was the vice, the obscenity, the reality of

161

London. It was lurid in the mixed evening light. Lamps were being lit . . . She stopped the cab opposite a little row of posts in an alley. She got out and made her way into the Square.

The sound of the traffic was dulled. It was very silent here. In the October afternoon, with dead leaves falling, the old faded Square looked dingy and decrepit and full of mist. The houses were let out in offices, to societies, to people whose names were pinned up on the door-posts. The whole neighbourhood seemed to her foreign and sinister. She came to the old Queen Anne doorway with its heavy carved eyebrows and pressed the bell at the top of six or seven bells.

Since the slums are one of the areas of London which have changed most over the past century, it is important to an understanding of Virginia's work that we know which places she regarded as slums. The three most surprising are Notting Hill Gate, Covent Garden and Fulham, which are all nowadays desirable places to live. Of the other districts most have been invaded by the middle classes, particularly those close to the centre, such as Clerkenwell, Caledonian Road and Kentish Town. Even places slightly further afield, like Acton, Holloway, Kensal Rise, Walworth, Whitechapel, Bermondsey, Hoxton, Shoreditch and Wandsworth, are no longer considered slums as they were by Virginia.

Monuments

If Virginia liked the idea rather than the reality of London slums, she genuinely loved its monuments. She never tired of visiting and writing about even the most obvious of them. To that extent she was the perennial tourist.

St Paul's Cathedral

St Paul's alone justified living in London for Virginia, an opinion shared by Jacob in *Jacob's Room*. When Jacob's friend Cruttenden, who lives in Paris, attacks London Jacob defends it quite simply: 'There St Paul's'. Like Jacob, Virginia was fond of visiting St Paul's and lingering inside:

> Dim it is, haunted by ghosts of white marble, to whom the organ for ever chaunts. If a boot creaks, it's awful; then the order; the discipline. The verger with his rod has life ironed out beneath him. Sweet and holy are the angelic choristers. And for ever round the marble shoulders, in and out of the folded fingers, go the thin high sounds of voice and organ. For ever requiem — repose.

Martin Pargiter, in *The Years*, meeting his cousin Sally outside St Paul's, is impressed by his glimpse of the interior but even more affected by the exterior. As he looks up at the great dome 'all the weights in his body seemed to shift. He had a curious sense of something moving in his body in harmony with the building'. So excited is he by this change of proportion, he wishes he had been an architect. Virginia shared this feeling, but since she was a writer not an architect, she did her best with words and imagery to convey what St Paul's means to her. If there is such a thing as a shell secreted by man to fit man himself, she argues, we can find it in the City 'where the great streets join and St Paul's Cathedral, like the volute on the top of the snail's shell finishes it off'. In an equally fanciful metaphor she has Bernard describe St Paul's towards the end of *The Waves* as 'the brooding hen with spread wings from whose shelter run omnibuses and streams of men and women at the rush hour'. At other times Virginia

sees St Paul's as a great grey bubble. Her favourite view
of the vast cathedral was from Waterloo Bridge, where it
rose above the buildings that surrounded it. She would
have been shocked and saddened by the modern buildings
which obscure so many views of St Paul's today.

Westminster Abbey

From Waterloo Bridge Virginia could also see St Paul's'
great rival, Westminster Abbey, lying on the opposite side
of London. She has less to say about the Abbey, though
she does set a memorable scene from *Mrs Dalloway* there,
when Miss Kilman seeks refuge from her own resentments
and inadequacies. Perhaps Virginia found the Abbey and
neighbouring Houses of Parliament too regular a type of
beauty. She was certainly attracted by their opposite, the
kind of bizarre contrasts she saw in Covent Garden
between the costermongers' barrows and the grand Opera
House, or between the serenity of St Paul's and the busy
city offices that surrounded it. She saw other differences
between St Paul's and Westminster Abbey which may
also help to explain her preference for the former:

> Far from being spacious and serene, the Abbey is
> narrow and pointed, worn, restless and animated. One
> feels as if one had stepped from the democratic helter
> skelter, the hubbub and hum-drum of the street, into
> a brilliant assembly, a select society of men and women
> of the highest distinction.

Architecturally Virginia could appreciate the beauty of
Westminster Abbey, in particular the way the fine fans
of stone spread themselves across the ceiling, but it seemed to her a cold loveliness like bare boughs withered of
all their leaves. It may have been that the Abbey was too

privileged or exclusive for her taste. It may simply have
been that she had grown to prefer St Paul's through long
familiarity, living as she did nearer to it. She was also fond
of the smaller City churches which surround the great
cathedral, especially St Mary-le-Bow and St Clement
Dane, both close neighbours of Clifford's Inn.

The British Museum

Virginia's other favourite among London landmarks was
the British Museum. Apart from the ten years at Richmond,
she had spent her adult life within walking distance of the
Museum and frequently used its library. There under the
great dome of the reading room, she felt both humbled and
inspired by the names of famous writers looking down at
her. During the chaos of the General Strike of 1926 she was
particularly appreciative of the refuge it offered:

> ... I to the Brit[ish] Mus[eum] ; where all was chill seren-
> ity, dignity and severity. Written up are the names of great
> men; and we all cower like mice nibbling crumbs in our
> most official discreet impersonal mood beneath. I like this
> dusty bookish atmosphere. Most of the readers seemed to
> have rubbed their noses off and written their eyes out. Yet
> they have a life they like — believe in the necessity of mak-
> ing books, I suppose: verify, collate, make up other books,
> for ever.

Four years later, while playfully planning her old age in her
diary, Virginia decided that her days would be spent in this
great library. The very words 'British Museum' conjured up
for her a visual image and a whole state of mind. When Jacob
Flanders goes to study Marlowe there, the author of *Jacob's
Room* asks us to consider that 'Plato is there cheek by jowl
with Aristotle; and Shakespeare with Marlowe. This great
mind is hoarded beyond the power of any single mind to

possess it. . . . And then there is science, pictures, architecture,—an enormous mind.' When Virginia stood under
the great dome in imagination in *A Room of One's Own*,
she felt as if she were 'a thought in the huge bald forehead'.
More frivolously, she enjoyed the eccentric characters she
saw in the library and immortalised a few of them in
Jacob's Room: Miss Marchmont, who believed that colour
is sound, Fraser, the atheist, and Miss Julia Hedges, the
feminist. Above all, however, Virginia loved the British
Museum because it represented the point where all knowledge was gathered together.

Buckingham Palace

Away from her favourite spots Virginia's imagination
flags a little. Buckingham Palace, for instance, is seen not
very subtly as a symbol of all the pomp and ceremony of
royalty. As the poor people of Pimlico wait for the royal
car to arrive in *Mrs Dalloway*, we are given only the most
superficial view of Nash's famous façade: the flag flying,
the statue of Queen Victoria 'billowing on her mound' the
fountain, the banks of geraniums. Clearly Virginia's imagination is not stimulated as much by Buckingham Palace as
it is by St Paul's or the British Museum. There are no vivid
metaphors of voluted snail-shells, huge bald foreheads or
brooding hens here.

The Houses of Parliament

The same is true of the Houses of Parliament. Whilst
Virginia admires their splendour, she is curiously
lukewarm in her description of them. When commissioned
to write about London for *Ideal Home*, she chose the House
of Commons for one of her five subjects, but more from a

sense of duty than love, one suspects. What stimulated
her most was the idea of an imaginary debate of the nineteenth century and an actual debate in the twentieth,
illustrating the greatness of the past and the smallness of
the present. The magnificence of Parliament's
Westminster Hall interests her only as a symbol of the
difference between an aristocratic and a democratic age.
Since Virginia was not particularly fond of the Houses
of Parliament, they do not figure largely in her work,
apart from Big Ben, which fascinates her. It is an obvious
device for letting us know the time in such novels as
Night and Day, where Mary Datchett, waiting for her
guests to arrive, hears the 'nine mellow strokes . . . a message from the great clock at Westminster'. More significantly Big Ben is also used to help shape the flow of the
stream-of-consciousness technique in *Mrs Dalloway* (which
was originally called *The Hours*). As Clarissa Dalloway
goes to buy her flowers, Septimus pays his fatal visit to
Sir William Bradshaw, Peter visits first Clarissa, then
Regent's Park, Richard keeps his luncheon appointment
with Lady Bruton, Septimus leaps from his window
and Clarissa finally holds her party, their mass of disparate
thoughts jumping about in time are structured and linked
partly by the striking of Big Ben. In addition the strokes
themselves seem to hold an almost mystical meaning for
Clarissa, as for Virginia:

> For having lived in Westminster—how many years now?
> over twenty,—one feels even in the midst of the traffic,
> or waking at night, Clarissa was positive, a particular
> hush, or solemnity; an indescribable pause; a suspense
> . . . before Big Ben strikes. There! Out it boomed. First
> a warning, musical; then the hour, irrevocable. The
> leaden circles dissolved in the air.

In this instance, the striking of Big Ben leads Clarissa on

to think, as Virginia must have done, how much she loved life, particularly in London in June.

The River Thames

Linking all these landmarks and running through the centre of Virginia's writing is the Thames. Time and again her characters escape to the river. Some are suffering from bewilderment, like Ralph in *Night and Day* when he discovers Katharine's engagement to William; some are brimming over with joy, like the same Ralph when he eventually becomes engaged to Katharine himself; others, such as Helen Ambrose in *The Voyage Out*, faced with separation from her children, are in agony. All go to the river in states of extreme emotion, as though the river can in some way help. When Ralph wants to tell Katharine of his love for her, he turns off the Strand towards the river, where he can express his emotions more easily. The river also symbolizes, for Ralph at any rate, the unknown. Walking along the Embankment shortly after his discovery of Katharine's engagement to William, he reflects on his bleak future in imagery taken straight from the river:

> He made no pattern out of the sights he saw. He felt himself now, as he had often fancied other people, adrift on the stream, and far removed from any control of it, a man with no grasp upon circumstances any longer. . . . He sat himself down, in spite of the chilly fog which obscured the farther bank and left its lights suspended upon a blank surface, upon one of the riverside seats, and let the tide of disillusionment sweep through him. For the time being all bright points in his life were blotted out; all prominences levelled. . . . He rose, and looked into the river whose swift race of dun-

coloured waters seemed the very spirit of futility and oblivion.

At the end of *Night and Day* the river reflects the romance and poetry Ralph and Katharine have found to-gether: 'Pausing, they looked down in to the river which bore its dark tide of waters endlessly moving'.

Virginia herself loved the Thames, which she regularly crossed from 1905 to 1907 when she taught at the Work-ing Men's College in Waterloo Road, and again from 1914 to 1924, when her train from Richmond sometimes deposited her at Waterloo Station. It may have been famil-iarity which made her so fond of Waterloo Bridge, for she loved it above all others. Returning to Waterloo Station from Bloomsbury in November 1923 she felt such excite-ment as she crossed Waterloo Bridge it was as though she were writing Shakespeare (see page 141). This sense of significance was strengthened by the living history that surrounded her on Waterloo Bridge: to the east of St Paul's and all the City churches, to the west the Houses of Parliament, Westminster Abbey and the Disney-like towers of Old Scotland Yard. No wonder she felt 'an absurd visionary excitement' as she gazed at it all. In *Jacob's Room* she tries to explain the mystery she senses standing on Waterloo Bridge:

> The wind has blown up the waves. The river races beneath us, and the men standing on the barges have to lean all their weight on the tiller. A black tarpaulin is tied down over a swelling load of gold. Avalanches of coal glitter blackly. As usual, painters are slung on planks across the great riverside hotels, and the hotel windows have already points of light in them. On the other side the city is white as if with age; St Paul's swells white above the fretted, pointed, or oblong buildings beside it. The cross alone shines rosy-gilt.

But what century have we reached? Has this procession from the Surrey side to the Strand gone on for ever? That old man has been crossing the Bridge these six hundred years, with the rabble of little boys at his heels, for he is drunk, or blind with misery, and tied round with old clouts of clothing such as pilgrims might have worn. He shuffles on. No one stands still. It seems as if we marched to the sound of music; perhaps the wind and the river; perhaps these same drums and trumpets — the ecstasy and hubbub of the soul.

Beyond Waterloo Bridge and St Paul's, along Upper and Lower Thames Street, round the Tower of London, past Tower Bridge lie London's docks. Many of these are no longer in active use, though some, such as St Katharine's Docks, have been turned into residential areas. Even Wapping High Street, which was in Virginia's day a cobbled lane steaming with smells of malt and oil and blocked by waggons, is today a fashionable place to live and work. For Mr and Mrs Ambrose in *The Voyage Out* it was the start of a long sea-journey to South America (see page 124). Virginia is intensely aware of London's history in dockland and when writing her historical novel, *Orlando*, she has the aristocratic Orlando reveal the 'common' blood in his/her veins by visiting Wapping Old Stairs, where he chats to the sailors and flirts with the 'free' women he finds there.

Virginia likes to think of London's docks, for they represented the working side of London. And clearly her favourite parts of London are the busiest. She loves the contrast between its many beautiful buildings and the bustle of everyday activity that surrounds them, hence her preference for St Paul's over Westminster Abbey, for Waterloo Bridge over Westminster. With the docks her imagination is stimulated not only by their business, but also by their romance. She loves to think of the great sailing ships coming up past the North Foreland and the

Reculvers and entering the narrow waters of the Port of
London, continuing past the low banks of Gravesend
and Northfleet and Tilbury, up Erith Reach, Barking
Reach and Gallion's Reach, past the gas works and the
sewage works till they find a space reserved for them in
the deep waters of the Docks. She also loves to contem-
plate the wide variety of ships and cargoes that enter
London Docks, from tramp steamers and coal-barges to
vast liners, from humble bricks and cement from Harwich
and Colchester to the timber, iron, grain, wine, sugar,
paper, tallow and fruit that come from more exotic places:
'whatever the ship has gathered from the plains, from the
forests, from the pastures of the whole world is here lifted
from its hold and set in its right place'. The romance, it
seems, has an extremely practical base, as she herself
reminds us in *The London Scene*:

> A snake, a scorpion, a beetle, a lump of amber, the
> diseased tooth of an elephant, a basin of quicksilver —
> these are some of the rarities and oddities that have
> been picked out of this vast merchandise and stood on
> a table. But with this one concession to curiosity, the
> temper of the Docks is severely utilitarian.

London Parks

Having stressed Virginia's love of the practical, business
side of London, we are immediately faced with an
exception — London's parks. For there is no doubt that
Virginia greatly appreciated these. The West End parks —
St James's, Hyde Park and the Green Park she describes
mainly in 'the season', when she imagines them metaphor-
ically preparing themselves for the social round:

> Already in the morning before there was a chance of

171

a procession, the green chairs were ranged among the plump brown flower beds with their curled hyacinths, as if waiting for something to happen,—for a curtain to rise; for Queen Alexandra to come bowing through the gates.

Virginia is particularly interested in that 'bald scrubbed space by Marble Arch where Speakers congregate'. Martin and Sally Pargiter in *The Years*, linger to hear various speakers expounding their obsessions. They also see the riders cantering down the Row in Hyde Park. All is gaiety and freshness in Virginia's West End parks. In *Jacob's Room* Jacob and Bonamy sit watching the carriages and motor cars passing incessantly round Hyde Park and over the Serpentine Bridge. Clara Durrant, in the same book, passes the statue of Achilles near Park Lane, as she walks with Mr Bowling and her dog in Hyde Park. Of the Green Park Virginia has less to say, but in St James's she is at her most poetic. As Clarissa Dalloway enters St James's Park on her walk from Victoria Street to Bond Street, all is quiet content: 'the silence; the mist; the hum; the slow-swimming happy ducks; the pouched birds waddling'. By contrast, Regent's Park, where Septimus Smith waits for his appointment with the psychiatrist in the same book, seems noisy and less privileged. Instead of meeting the courtier Hugh Whitbread, as we did in St James's, we are introduced to Maisie Johnson, up in London from Edinburgh to take a post at her uncle's in Leadenhall, Carrie Dempster from Kentish Town, and Peter Walsh, who finds both Clarissa and Hugh snobbish. Yet Virginia was extremely fond of Regent's Park. Apart from Kensington Gardens, in which she had walked daily as a child, Regent's Park was the one Virginia knew best. During her twenty-six years in Bloomsbury it was the nearest escape and she went often. She walked there in all seasons, sometimes alone, sometimes with Leonard. One of her

favourite walks was by the lake. At times she fled there
to work off her angers and depressions and on such
occasions the treatment was so successful that instead of
rage she was flooded with ecstasy. Part of the ecstasy was
due to the 'blue and red mounds of flowers burning a wet
radiance through the green grey haze'. Whatever the cause,
the effect was always the same: she would begin making
up pages of stories. She had no doubt that the greatest
happiness in the world was walking through Regent's Park
on a 'green but wet — green but red-pink and blue evening
— the flower beds . . . emerging from the general mist —
and making up phrases'. When Clive Bell's ex-mistress,
Mary Hutchinson, went to live at 3 Prince Albert Road
Virginia on several occasions visited the Zoo after dinner
with Mary. The first time she enjoyed it greatly, the
second less so, though it was amusing to meet Lytton's
brother-in-law, Simon Bussy, in the reptile house with
two other Frenchmen. When another friend, Elizabeth
Bowen, the novelist, took a house at 2 Clarence Gate in
1935, Virginia told her that she often thought how nice
it would be to live beside Regent's Park.

However beautiful Virginia found London's parks, they
are not the most representative part of her London. As I
have tried to show, she preferred beauty which, as she
put it, 'came in by the back door', beauty which surprised
one by its incongruity or unexpectedness. It is rarely the
conventionally beautiful which delights her. She far
prefers the unplanned conjunctions of the working world.
When writing of the docks, she sums up what it is that
attracts her most in London:

> . . . the aptness of everything to its purpose, the fore-
> thought and readiness which have provided for every
> process, come, as if by the back door, to provide that
> element of beauty which nobody in the Docks has
> given half a second of thought to. The warehouse is

perfectly fit to be a warehouse; the crane to be a crane. Hence beauty begins to steal in. The cranes dip and swing, and there is rhythm in their regularity. The warehouse walls are open wide to admit sacks and barrels; but through them one sees all the roofs of London, its masts and spires, and the unconscious, vigorous movements of men lifting and unloading. Because barrels of wine require to be laid on their sides in cool vaults all the mystery of dim lights, all the beauty of low arches is thrown in as an extra.

This was written over twenty years after Roger Fry was forced to close his Omega Workshops through lack of finances, but the theory is very similar. Virginia was almost certainly influenced in her aesthetic principles by Roger Fry, Vanessa Bell and Duncan Grant, all of whom demonstrated in their work for Omega a belief that beauty emerges from the fitness of an object for its purpose.

4

Some Virginia Woolf Walks
Illustrations and Maps* by Tamsin Hickson

When Eleanor Pargiter is offered a lift home from a dinner
party by her brother-in-law René in *The Years*, she replies:
'No, I'll walk. I like walking in London'. It could have
been the author herself speaking, for Virginia loved walking, particularly in London. From her earliest years she
had been taken on long walks by her prodigiously
energetic father and, far from putting her off the exercise,
it seems to have become a necessary part of her life.

Of my suggested seven walks that follow, three are
based on Virginia's life, four on her writings. For those
who do not know Virginia's novels well, there is still a
great deal of interest to be had from these latter walks,
since each of them provides an excuse for seeing some of
London's most rewarding sights.

*For purposes of convenience the maps that follow are not drawn
strictly to scale.

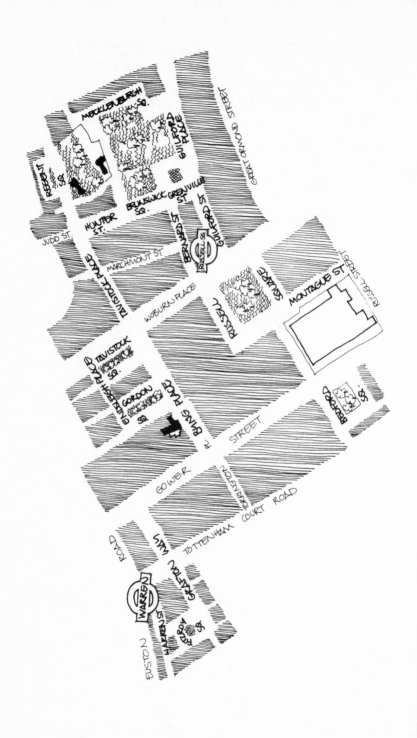

Walk 1

Bloomsbury Walk
The Houses of Virginia Woolf and
Some of Her Friends

A walk round Bloomsbury is always a pleasure, particularly if one is treading in the footsteps of the famous. In this
effort to recreate Virginia Woolf's Bloomsbury I have had
to choose between convenience and chronology. In order
to avoid a great deal of retracing of steps I have chosen
to introduce her houses as they fit into a pleasant walk,
not in the order in which she inhabited them. Not all the
houses survive in their original state, but most of the
squares she lived in are relatively unchanged and help us
to see what she saw as she took her daily walks.

Starting with the furthest she ever lived from her
personal centre of Bloomsbury, the first stop is 29 Fitzroy Square. Warren Street tube station is a convenient

place to begin this walk. Make your way down Warren Street and Fitzroy Street, noting that Vanessa Bell rented a large studio at the back of number 8 Fitzroy Street in 1929, and this will take you to Fitzroy Square. Number 29, in the south-west corner, was the second Bloomsbury dwelling of Virginia and her brother, Adrian Stephen, from 1907 to 1911. They moved here when their sister Vanessa married Clive Bell and took over their former family house at 46 Gordon Square.

Virginia and Adrian first became independent of their older sister here (their older brother Thoby had recently died) and began to entertain on their own account. They revived the 'Thursday evenings' started by Thoby at 46 Gordon Square and they also introduced regular Friday evening readings, of authors ranging from the Restoration dramatists and Shakespeare to Swinburne and Ibsen. It was in this house also that Lytton Strachey proposed to Virginia in 1909 and was accepted, though the engagement was extremely short-lived (Lytton withdrew his proposal the next day). When the lease expired at number 29, Virginia and Adrian moved to 38 Brunswick Square.

A few doors away from 29 Fitzroy Square, at number 22, Duncan Grant rented a studio in 1907 and the same year started to share a flat with Maynard Keynes at number 26. Duncan was always wandering in and out of Virginia and Adrian's house, often in borrowed clothes — in search of food! Even more excitingly, perhaps, it was at 33 Fitzroy Square that Roger Fry opened the Omega Workshops in 1913. Fry wanted to combine his interest in producing well-designed, decorated furniture and other artefacts with his desire to help some of his impecunious artist friends earn a living whilst leaving them time to continue with their own work. The Omega closed in 1919, a year after the end of the First World War, partly due to the effects of that war on the economy. Besides running the Omega from 33, Roger Fry also had a studio at number 21.

A friend, but not a member of the Bloomsbury Group, George Bernard Shaw, had lived at 29 Fitzroy Square with his mother from 1887 until he married Charlotte Payne-Townshend in 1898, and it was in this house that he established himself as a dramatist, by writing *Mrs Warren's Profession*, *Arms and the Man* and *Candida*.

Leaving Fitzroy Square by the south-east corner, walk along Grafton Way, cross Tottenham Court Road and turn right down Gower Street, noting number 10, where Lady Ottoline Morrell came to live in May 1927. She had recently given up Garsington, her famous country house where she and her politician husband, Philip, had entertained well-known writers and painters, including many of the Bloomsbury Group. Also turn into Bedford Square on your your right, to look at number 44, where the Morrells had lived before the First World War and where Virginia had sometimes visited the 'Ott's' Thursday evenings in about 1910 (see page 71).

After this slight detour, walk back up Gower Street until you reach Dillons Bookshop, then right along Torrington, Mallet and Byng Place to Gordon Square, which is on your left. Number 46, on the east side of the square, was the home of the Stephen  children after their father died in 1904, that is from 1905 to 1907. As I have already mentioned, Thoby Stephen started his famous Thursday evenings here, to which

Leonard Woolf was one of the first to be invited. Other regulars included Clive Bell, Desmond MacCarthy and Lytton Strachey. It was after Thoby died in 1906 and Vanessa married Clive Bell that Virginia left for Fitzroy Square—not too close, but not too far away.

Maynard Keynes also lived at number 46 Gordon Square, after Vanessa and Clive left it. Vanessa moved a few doors away to number 50, where she rented the upper half of the house from her brother Adrian in 1920. When she left in 1922 Clive Bell took over the flat at number 50 and Vanessa moved to number 37 for the next seven years, that is 1922-29.

In the same square, at number 51, Lytton Strachey lived from 1909 with his family until they moved out of Bloomsbury to Belsize Park Gardens. Lytton's brother, James, lived at number 41 Gordon Square from 1919 until 1956 with Alix Sargant Florence. From 1926 they shared the house during the week with Ralph Partridge, who had married Dora Carrington, and Ralph's mistress Frances Marshall. At weekends Ralph went home to his wife, who lived with Lytton Strachey at Ham Spray during the 1920s.

At the north end of Gordon Square, in which was originally 6 Gordon (now Endsleigh) Place, lived Raymond Mortimer, one of the younger, fringe members of Bloomsbury.

Now return to the south end of Gordon Square and walk eastwards to the adjoining Tavistock Square. Number 52 Tavistock Square, which was three houses from Southampton Row on the south side, was destroyed in the Second World War and replaced by part of the Tavistock Hotel. However, houses very similar to it still stand on the west side of the square. Number 52 was the most important of all Virginia's London houses. She and Leonard moved here in 1924, when Virginia was beginning to feel exiled in Richmond and desperate to get back

to central London. They remained here until the outbreak
of war in 1939, when they felt it necessary to find a
longer lease and a less devastated area at 37 Mecklenburgh
Square. At 52 Tavistock Square Virginia and Leonard's
publishing house, the Hogarth Press, occupied the
rambling basement, which also contained a converted
billiard-room under the garden for Virginia to write in.
The Woolfs' living accommodation was on the top two
floors of the five-storied house, and the intervening two
floors were let to a firm of solicitors, Dolman and
Pritchard. The relationship must have been an harmon-
ious one, for when the Woolfs moved to Mecklenburgh
Square, Dolman and Pritchard moved with them.

On the east side of Tavistock Square, which is generally
thought of as Woburn Place, lived Charles Dickens at
Tavistock House, now the (rebuilt) home of the British
Medical Association. Dickens lived there from 1851 till
he left for Gad's Hill, Kent, in 1860. At Tavistock House
he wrote *Bleak House* (1852-53), *Hard Times* (1854), *A
Tale of Two Cities* (1859) and started *Great Expectations*
(1860-61).

Now walk down Tavistock Square and turn left into
Tavistock Place. Cross Marchmont Street and the meeting
point of Judd and Hunter Streets until you reach Regent
Square. Here, at number 36, which has since been
replaced by council flats, Vanessa lived during 1919,
having taken over the lease of a flat from James Strachey
when he moved to 41 Gordon Square. You can see what
her house would have looked like from the few remaining
originals on the south side of the square.

Retracing your steps westwards to Hunter Street, turn
left down it to Brunswick Square. On your left, occupy-
ing almost the whole of the north side, is the School of
Pharmacy, which stands on the site of Virginia's third
Bloomsbury home, number 38 Brunswick Square.
(Virginia and Adrian moved here after they left Fitzroy

Square in 1911.) Next door at number 40, was the old
Foundling Hospital, which still stands, renamed The
Coram Trust. Virginia joked that the Foundling Hospital
should console her very respectable female relatives who
disapproved of her sharing a house, unchaperoned, with
young men. Apart from her brother, there were Maynard
Keynes, Duncan Grant and Leonard Woolf, who
proposed to Virginia while they were both living here.
Number 38 itself was pulled down about 1936 to make
was for the School of Pharmacy. If you walk down the
alley between the east end of the School of Pharmacy
and the Coram Trust, you can see the old burial ground
which Virginia's house and the Foundling Hospital over-
looked. The west side of Brunswick Square, badly bombed in the war, was cleared in the 1970s to make way for
the Brunswick Shopping Centre. When Virginia accepted
Leonard in 1912 they left to be married and found lodgings at Clifford's Inn from 1912 to 1914. From 1914 to
1924 they lived mainly in Richmond, before taking their
house at 52 Tavistock Square. Another member of
Bloomsbury, the novelist, E.M. Forster, lived at number
26 Brunswick Square from 1929 to 1939. Perhaps the
most entertaining description of Brunswick Square —
which is really a double square, with Mecklenburgh to its
east — comes in Jane Austen's *Emma*, where Emma's
sister, Isabella, gives a spirited defence of the healthiness
of Brunswick Square to her hypochondriac father:

'No, indeed — *we* are not at all in a bad air. Our part of
London is so very superior to most others! — You
must not confound us with London in general, my
dear sir. The neighbourhood of Brunswick Square is
very different from almost all the rest. We are so very
airy! I should be unwilling, I own, to live in any other
part of the town; — there is hardly any other that I
could be satisfied to have my children in: — but *we* are

so remarkably airy!—Mr Wingfield thinks the vicinity
of Brunswick Square decidedly the most favourable
as to air.'

From the north-east corner of the square, you can
walk through a small alley-way, past a nursery-school, to
Mecklenburgh Square, where Virginia and Leonard lived
—or rather camped—at number 37 from 1939 to 1940.
When the house was bombed in 1940, they moved per-
manently to their country house, Monk House at Rodmell,
near Lewes, Sussex, and moved the Hogarth Press to
Letchworth. Number 37 Mecklenburgh Square turned out
to be Virginia's last London house, for in March 1941 she
decided to end her life. The section on the north side of
Mecklenburgh Square where number 37 was situated, has
been carefully rebuilt though not exactly as it was. The
William Goodenough House now occupies the site of 37,
but some of the original houses, with their imposing
entrances, still survive on the north side next to Coram's
Fields and give one a very close idea of what Virginia and
Leonard's house looked like.

If you have any energy left you should leave Mecklenburgh Square by way of Guilford Street, turning right
into Grenville Street, then left into Bernard Street. At
number 42 lived Roger Fry with his mistress, Helen Anrep
in the 1920s. At the end of Bernard Street is Russell
Square, which will take you to Montague Place and the
British Museum. Virginia spent a lot of her time here and
is probably revealing her own feelings quite closely when
she described Jacob sitting studiously there in *Jacob's
Room* (see above page 165).

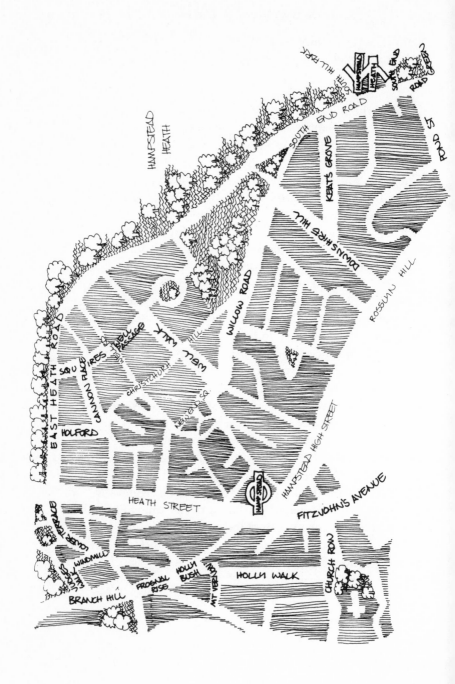

Walk 2

Hampstead Walk

Hampstead is another area in which Virginia enjoyed walking and, since she and Leonard had a number of friends there, quite often did so.

The easiest way to cover this walk, except on a Sunday when parking restrictions are lifted, is to take the Northern line tube to Hampstead. Once out of the station, walk south down Heath Street until you reach on your right Church Row with its magnificent eighteenth-century houses. Number 28 Church Row is where Leonard, sometimes accompanied by Virginia, visited Margaret Llewelyn Davies and her friend Lilian Harris to discuss their work for the Women's Co-operative Guild.

Virginia had got to know Margaret through another Hampstead friend, her Greek teacher, Janet Case, whose house is within easy walking distance of Church Row. To reach it you must turn down Holly Walk, which is half-way along Church Row on the north side. When you reach Mount Vernon, turn right into Holly Bush Place. Then walk north up Frognal Rise into Branch Hill and continue up until you reach Judges Walk on your right. Go along Judges Walk until you reach Windmill Hill, also on your right. At number 5 lived Janet Case with her sister Emphie, whom Virginia satirised in a letter to Vanessa (see page 159).

Another friend Virginia visited in Hampstead, before her early death, was Katherine Mansfield, who lived with her husband John Middleton Murry at 2 Portland Villas. To reach this squat little house, known jokingly as 'the elephant' because of its ungainly shape, you must continue to the end of Windmill Hill, emerging at Lower Terrace. Turn left here and walk up to the main road, that is, the junction of Heath Street and North End Way at

Whitestone Pond. Cross this main road to East Heath Road, which leads down to the Middleton Murrys' house on the right just past Squires Mount. Originally 2 Portland Villas, this house has since been re-addressed as 17 East Heath Road. A blue plaque remains to commemmorate the writers' time there. Since East Heath Road is rather narrow and noisy at this point, it is probably preferable to retrace your steps a few yards to Squires Mount, cross Well Road at a slight diagonal and continue along Well Passage until you reach Well Walk, where Margaret Llewelyn Davies and Lilian Harris had their second

Well Passage

Hampstead home at number 26. They continued to be visited by Leonard, sometimes accompanied by Virginia. It is interesting to remember that Keats moved to number 1 Well Walk in 1817 with his two brothers. The house has since been demolished, but it is still possible to visit Keats's other, more famous, house in Keats' Grove, which Virginia herself visited and described at some length. To reach Keats' Grove (Formerly Wentworth Place) turn left into Willow Road at the end of Well Walk. Just before Willow Road meets Hampstead Heath turn right up Downshire Hill until you reach the church, then turn left into Keats' Grove. Here you can visit Keats's house with a copy of Virginia's essay, 'Great Men's Houses' (*The London*

Scene (London, 1982) in your hand and imagine with her
how it must have seemed to Keats in 1819:

> . . . if Keats left any impress upon his house it is the
> impression not of fever, but of that clarity and
> dignity which come from order and self-control. The
> rooms are small but shapely; downstairs the long
> windows are so large that half the wall sems made of
> light. Two chairs turned together are close to the
> window as if someone had sat there reading and had
> just got up and left the room. The figure of the reader
> must have been splashed with shade and sun as the
> hanging leaves stirred in the breeze. Birds must have
> hopped close to his foot. The room is empty save for
> the two chairs, for Keats had few possessions, little
> furniture and not more, he said, than one hundred and
> fifty books. And perhaps it is because the rooms are
> so empty and furnished with light and shadow than
> with chairs and tables that one does not think of
> people, here where so many people have lived. The
> imagination does not evoke scenes. It does not strike
> one that there must have been eating and drinking here;
> people must have come in and out; they must have put
> down bags, left parcels; they must have scrubbed and
> cleaned and done battle with dirt and disorder and
> carried cans of water from the basement to the bed-
> rooms. All the traffic of life is silenced. The voice of
> the house is the voice of leaves brushing in the wind;
> of branches stirring in the garden. Only one presence—
> that of Keats himself—dwells here.

When you come out of Keats's house turn right towards
the Heath and right again into South End Road, which
will take you down to South End Green. The 'Pizza Place'
here was once the bookshop which George Orwell worked in and made famous in *Keep the Aspidistra Flying*

(1936). Orwell himself lived above the bookshop in Warwick Mansions, Pond Street. A little further up the same street, at number 6, lived the Hon. Dorothy Brett,

Well Walk

a close friend of the D.H. Lawrences and Middleton Murrys. Virginia visited 6 Pond Street on several occasions when she attended Brett's Thursday 'evenings', but she so disliked the Hampstead 'types' she met there that she soon stopped going.

You have now completed your walk, but if you have still some energy left, you should return to South End Green, walk up South Hill and Parliament Hill, and make your way across the Heath to Ken Wood, as Virginia and Leonard often did.

Walk 3

Virginia's City Walk
(approximately one hour)

Of all the places Virginia loved walking, the City was
probably her favourite. When in London she walked there
almost every day. Once exiled to Monk's House by the
war in 1940, she thought 'with what is love, I suppose,
of the City: of the walk to the Tower; that is my
England; . . .'

Though the walk to the Tower was Virginia's favourite, she had others, which she varied according to her
mood. Sometimes she would wander from Wapping Old
Stairs through Shadwell and Whitechapel; at others she
would explore Leather Lane, Neville's Court and the Cut
with its smells of stale fish. On one occasion she walked
from the Savoy along the Embankment to Blackfriars, then
on to Upper Thames Street and Cannon Street before taking
a bus home. She was always discovering new corners of the
ancient City; in 1937 she found the Wren church of St
James Garlickhithe, on the corner of Garlick Hill and Upper
Thames Street, then walked back via the south bank of the
Thames to St Mary's, near Lambeth Palace.

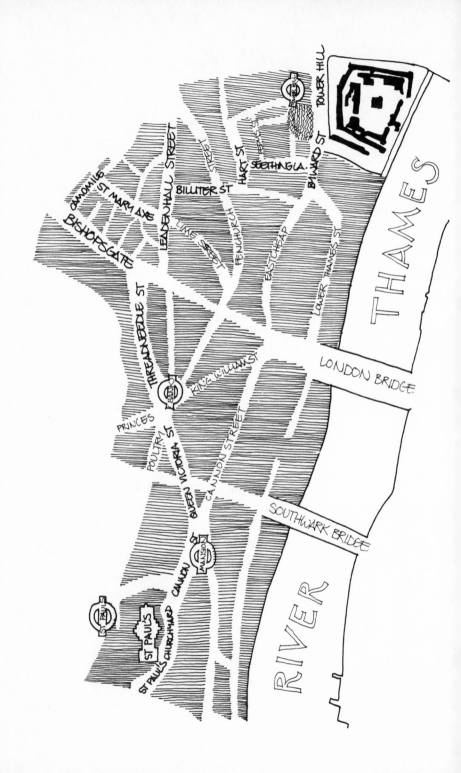

However, for this City walk I have chosen Virginia's favourite, her walk from Fleet Street to the Tower of London, a walk she promised to take Vita Sackville-West on in 1937:

> ... I'll take you to the Tower—I've just been there, this dripping Sunday; because almost every day I take my walk through the City. I like it better than Kent— Bread Street, Camomile Street, Seething Lane, All Hallows, St Olaves—Then out one comes at The Tower and there I walk on the terrace by the guns, with the ships coming up or down—which is it? ...

Virginia probably walked all the way from Bloomsbury to the City, but since few people share her walking abilities, I suggest you first take a bus or tube to St Paul's Cathedral. Start by walking along St Paul's Churchyard, which is the name of a road, until you reach Cannon Street. Taking note of Bread Street on your left, a name that obviously caught Virginia's imagination, carry on

Corner of the Bank of England, Threadneedle Street and the Royal Exchange

down Cannon Street to Mansion House tube station,
where you should turn half-left into Queen Victoria Street,
noting another name, Poultry. which Virginia would have
relished. Queen Victoria Street will take you to the
magnificent complex of the Bank of England on your
left, the Royal Exchange straight ahead and the Mansion
House on your right.

After taking in all this splendour you should go straight
on, between the Bank and the Royal Exchange up Threadneedle Street, another name Virginia would have appreciated. When you reach Bishopsgate at the end of Threadneedle Street, turn left into it, cross the road and carry
on, past St Helen's Place, if you can resist it, to
Camomile Street, another of Virginia's favourite street-
names. In fact St Helen's churchyard, which you will pass
again as you descend Camomile Street, is an attractive
place to stop for breath, or lunch if you've brought it
with you.

At the end of Camomile Street, you need to turn right
into St Mary Axe, which will take you south to Leadenhall Street. Turn left along Leadenhall Street until you
reach Billiter Street, which you must cross, and almost
immediately opposite you is Mark Lane. Half-way down
Mark Lane on your left is Hart Street, which leads to
one of the two churches Virginia mentions in her letter
to Vita, St Olave's, an ancient City building well worth
a visit. Turn right at the church into Seething Lane.
Apart from being referred to specifically by Virginia
Seething Lane is also of interest as the site of the Navy
Office in which Samuel Pepys worked. Destroyed by
fire in 1673, only seven years after the Great Fire, it is
commemorated by a plaque in the small garden square.
Seething Lane takes you to Byward Street and the second
church mentioned by Virginia, All Hallow's. (There is
another All Hallow's by London Wall, but it is obviously
not the one Virginia meant.)

Once at All Hallow's, you will see the Tower of London to your east. You will be able to get down to the river and on the terrace by the guns as Virginia did, though it is unlikely that you will see as many ships coming up and down as she did.

The Tower of London

You will probably want to take a bus or tube home. Even Virginia felt the need of public transport home from the Tower. Tower Hill is the nearest underground station, and the number 15 bus will take you straight back to Central London.

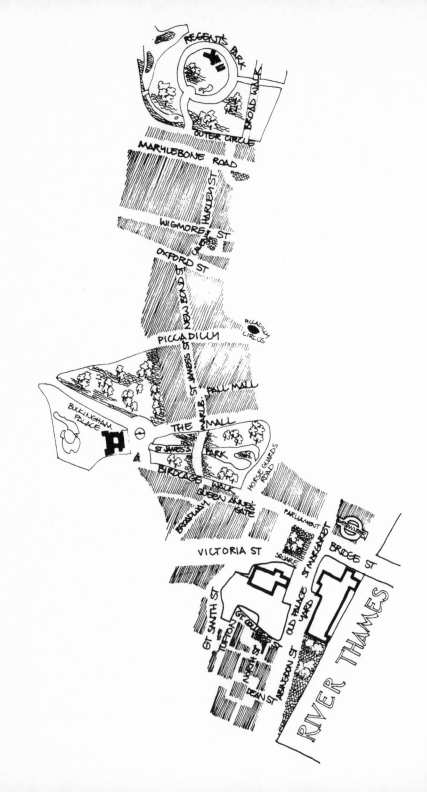

Walk 4

A Mrs Dalloway Walk
(from Westminster to Regent's Park)

The best place to start a Mrs Dalloway walk is at Westminster tube station. Here you can wait for Big Ben to
strike and feel, as Clarissa Dalloway did, after living in
Westminster for twenty years, 'a particular hush, or
solemnity; an indescribable pause; a suspense . . . before
Big Ben strikes. There! Out it boomed. First a warning,
musical; then the hour, irrevocable. The leaden circles
dissolved in the air'. If you walk towards Parliament
Square, cross Bridge Street and continue along Margaret
Place you will pass the Houses of Parliament on your
left and arrive at Victoria Tower
Gardens. (Here, incidentally, it is
worth a small digression into the
Gardens to see Rodin's 'The
Burghers of Calais'.) Carry on
along Abingdon Street until you
reach Dean Stanley Street, the
third on your right. This will take
you to Smith Square, where you
can, if you have time, visit St
John's Concert Hall. Follow Lord
North Street out of the square
on your right, crossing Peter Street,
and turn left at the top of Lord
North Street into Cowley Street,
then right into Barton Street. It is
in one of these four streets, I believe,

Clarissa to have lived, from a number of hints given in *Mrs
Dalloway*. Richard Dalloway returns home from lunch
with Lady Bruton through the nearby Dean's Yard,
Clarissa hears Big Ben booming out the hours, and her
first stop on her trip to buy flowers in Bond Street is on

the curb of Victoria Street, which is the nearest large
thoroughfare. Virginia's diary of January 1923 shows
her admiring a house in Barton Street, which was unfortunately too expensive to rent. She would at this time
have been planning *Mrs Dalloway*. Clarissa, then, may
well have come out of a house in Barton Street and turned left at the top into Great College Street. You might
like to explore Dean's Yard, which Richard Dalloway
used as a short cut, before following Tufton Street to
Little Smith Street. At the top of Little Smith Street
turn right into Great Smith Street and you will arrive at
Victoria Street, as Clarissa did. Unfortunately a great
deal of rebuilding has taken place at this end of the
street, but if you cross and turn left along it towards
Victoria Street, you will see some of the buildings
Clarissa saw that sparkling morning in June and perhaps
feel as she did about the area (see pages 9-10).

At Broadway, where you turn right, you will catch a
glimpse of the, unfortunately rebuilt, Army and Navy
Stores, where Elizabeth and Mrs Kilman had tea before
Elizabeth caught her number 11 bus from Victoria Street
to Fleet Street. At the top of Broadway you must cross
Tothill Street and follow Carteret Street down to Queen
Anne's Gate. Here you turn left, approaching Birdcage
Walk by the Gate itself. St James's Park and the entrance
to it lies straight ahead of you. 'But how strange on
entering the Park,' Clarissa thought, 'the silence; the mist;
the slow-swimming happy ducks; the pouched birds
waddling . . .' The pelicans and ducks are still there, and
if you stand on the bridge which spans the lake you will
see, to your left, Buckingham Palace and, to your right,
Whitehall Palace and other Government buildings. It was
from one of the latter that Clarissa saw Hugh Whitbread
bustling, carrying a dispatch-box, stamped with the
Royal Arms, on his way to the Palace.

If you're beginning to need refreshment, you may like

to take another small digression on your way out of St
James's Park to the Cake House on your right which
did not exist in Clarissa's day. If not, then you should
carry on out of the Park, cross the Mall and walk up
Marlborough Street along the side of St James's Palace,
a building of Tudor origin. A left turn at Pall Mall will
bring you to the bottom of St James's Street and its famous
gentlemen's clubs. It was in one of these clubs, when the
mysterious royal car passed by on its way from Bond
Street, that:

> Tall men, men of robust physique, well-dressed men
> with their tail-coats and their white slips and their
> hair raked back, who, for reasons difficult to discrim-
> inate, were standing in the bow window of White's
> with their hands behind the tails of their coats, look-
> ing out, perceived instinctively that greatness was
> passing, and the pale light of the immortal presence
> fell upon them as it had fallen upon Clarissa Dalloway.
> At once they stood even straighter, and removed their
> hands, and seemed ready to attend their Sovereign, if
> need be, to the cannon's mouth, as their ancestors had
> done before them. The white busts and the little tables
> in the background covered with copies of the *Tatler*
> and bottles of soda water seemed to approve . . .

White's is at the top of St James's Street on the right,
just past another famous club, Boodle's.

You have now reached Piccadilly, where Clarissa turns
right towards Hatchards bookshop, a slight digression on
her way to Bond Street. It is fascinating to know what
she saw in Hatchards' window. Apart from Shakespeare,
there were *Jorrocks' Jaunts and Jollities*, *Soapy Sponge*,
Mrs Asquith's *Memoirs* and *Big Game Shooting in Nigeria*.
Clarissa then turns and walks back towards Bond Street,
which is on the opposite side of Piccadilly. It is obvious

from Virginia's description that Clarissa is in her element
in this fashionable street, which brings out not only her
snobbishness but her strong aesthetic sense too:

> Bond Street fascinated her; Bond Street early in the
> morning in the season; its flags flying; its shops; no
> splash; no glitter; one roll of tweed in the shop where
> her father had bought his suits for fifty years; a few
> pearls; salmon on an iceblock.

There are no longer any flower-shops in Bond Street,
nor is there a fishmongers, but there is still at least one
shop where Clarissa's father might have bought tweed
for his suits and a number of jewellers, such as Cartiers,
where Clarissa could have bought her pearls. There is
definitely more 'splash' and 'glitter' than there used to
be. However, Bond Street remains fairly exclusive, as a
random count of the Bentleys and Rolls Royces parked
there shows.

It was here, in Old Bond Street, that Clarissa and
Septimus heard the royal car backfire. Septimus was on
his way up Bond Street to Harley Street, where he had
an appointment with Sir William Bradshaw. Clarissa too
walked on up Bond Street at least as far as Brook Street,
where she stopped to let a car pass. It was in Brook
Street, too, that Lady Bruton (her name taken perhaps
from nearby Bruton Street?) gave lunch to Richard
Dalloway and Hugh Whitbread that same day, in
return for advice over a letter to *The Times*.

If you cross Brook Street and continue up New Bond
Street you will reach Oxford Street, where Hugh stops
to look at shoes and socks on his way to Lady Bruton's.
Septimus and his wife Rezia also cross Oxford Street on
their way to Harley Street, probably going via Vere
Street, Henrietta Place and Cavendish Square.

It was in Harley Street that Septimus and Rezia paid

their memorable visit to the psychiatrist, Sir William Bradshaw. As you walk up Harley Street, note the vast number of brass plates advertising the many consultants who practise there, and do not forget to look out for Sir

Harley Street looking towards Regent's Park

William's low, powerful, grey car which so suited his grey life. At the top of Harley Street, turn right and cross the Marylebone Road to Park Square West, which will take you into Regent's Park, where Septimus and Rezia waited to keep their appointment with Sir William. There in the Broad Walk, slightly to your right, Septimus had his visions and Peter Walsh sat and watched the small child running into Rezia. If you still have the energy, return to Marylebone Road the way you came and turn left past Regent's Park tube station, where the old beggar-woman sang, and walk along Euston Road to Tottenham Court Road, off which Septimus and Rezia had their humble lodgings.

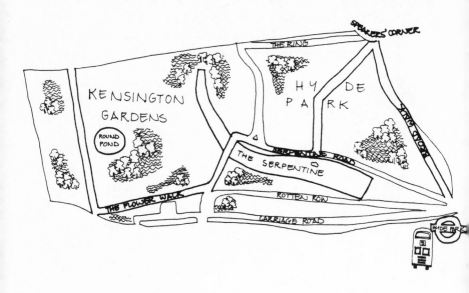

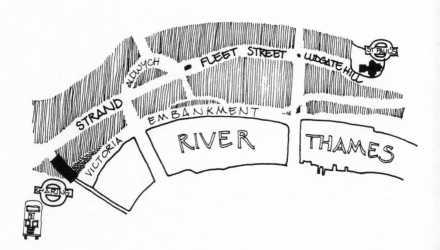

Walk 5

Martin and Sally Pargiter's Walk
(from *The Years*)

Martin Pargiter, who is visiting his stockbrokers in the
City, meets his eccentric cousin, Sally, by chance outside St Paul's Cathedral and invites her for lunch in a
nearby chop-house, which is how you might start this
walk. The Cock Tavern at 22 Fleet Street is a suitable
place, since Leonard and Virginia used to eat there daily
while living at Clifford's Inn. When Sally starts talking
rather wildly after lunch Martin decides that it is time
to leave the restaurant and accompanies her to the Round
Pond in Kensington Gardens, partly on foot, partly by
bus.

They begin their walk proper, as you should, from St
Paul's, which makes Martin wish he had been an architect
(see page 163). Descending Ludgate Hill they cross
Ludgate Circus and walk along Fleet Street, which was

obviously as crowded
then as now: 'Conver-
sation was impossible.
The pavement was so
narrow that he had to
step off and on in order
to keep beside her'.
When they reach Temple
Bar, which marks the
boundary between the
City of London and the
City of Westminster,
between Fleet Street
and the Strand, Martin
stops to point out to
Sally 'the splayed-out
figure at Temple Bar;

Temple Bar

it looked ridiculous as usual—something between a ser-
pent and a fowl. . . . They paused for a moment to look
at the little flattened figures lodged so uncomfortably
against the pediment of Temple Bar: Queen Victoria:
King Edward'.

As Martin and Sally walked on past the Law Courts
(the Royal Courts of Justice) they see men in wigs and
gowns scurrying in and out, some with red bags, some
with blue, and Martin thinks of his brother, Morris, who
has become a barrister. Having passed this 'cold mass of
decorated stone', Martin guides Sally along the Strand,
which is as noisy as Fleet Street and equally impossible
to talk in. The sight of a beggar-woman with no nose
makes him uneasy and he suddenly suggests they catch a
bus. So at Charing Cross station, which was 'like the piers
of a bridge; men and women were sucked in instead of
water'—they wait for a number 9 to take them to Hyde
Park. Allowing for today's one-way traffic system, their
route must have been through Trafalgar Square, into
Pall Mall, then into Waterloo Place and up Lower Regent
Street.

Once in Piccadilly Martin points out his father's club,
probably the Junior Army and Navy Club (known as
the 'In and Out'). He notes the sun blazing on the
windows of St George's Hospital and wonders why it
fills Sally with rapture, then helps her off the bus at
Hyde Park Corner. They cross the road to Hyde Park,
but you would be well advised to use the subway nowadays.

The scene at Hyde Park has changed since Martin
viewed it on his way to St Paul's from Ebury Street in
the morning:

> There were more cars; more women in pale summer
> dresses; more men in tail-coats and grey top-hats.
> The procession through the gates into the park was

beginning. Everyone looked festive. Even the little
dressmakers' apprentices with band-boxes looked as
if they were taking part in some ceremonial. Green
chairs were drawn up at the edge of the Row [i.e.
Rotten Row]. They were full of people looking
about them as if they had taken seats at a play. Riders
cantered to the end of the Row; pulled up their horses;
turned and cantered the other way. The wind, coming
from the west, moved white clouds grained with gold
across the sky. The windows of Park Lane shone with
blue and gold reflections.

Distracted by their conversation about Sally's sister
Maggie, who has married a Frenchman, Martin and Sally
take the wrong path. Instead of walking north-west
across Hyde Park to the Round Pond in Kensington
Gardens, they keep almost directly north up the Broad
Walk, parallel with Park Lane, and end up at Speakers'
Corner. Neither of them mind much, indeed they stay
to listen to the speakers until they remember Sally's
appointment with her sister at 4 p.m. Crossing Hyde
Park in a south-westerly direction, they arrive at the
Serpentine and follow it westwards until they reach the
bridge, which they cross into Kensington Gardens. Choosing the Flower Walk, which Virginia knew very well from
her childhood, they then climb the Broad Walk with its
view of Kensington Palace and the 'phantom church'
(that is St Mary Abbot's at the bottom of Kensington
Church Street) and reach the Round Pond on their
right. Martin admires the scene:

It was admirably composed. There was the white
figure of Queen Victoria against a green bank;
beyond, was the red brick of the old palace; the
phantom church raised its spire, and the Round Pond
made a pool of blue. A race of yachts was going

forward. The boats leaned on their sides so that the sails touched the water. There was a nice little breeze.

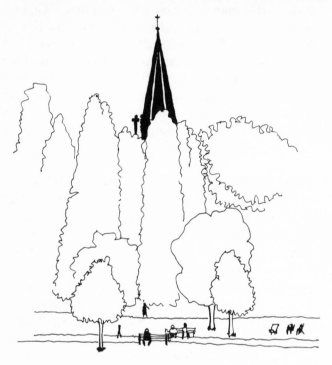

The 'Phantom Church'

This is technically the end of your walk, but it would be sad to leave the area without visiting Virginia's birthplace, which is only a few minutes' walk away. So, if you have the energy, go down the Broad Walk to Palace Gate. On your way, you will pass an ancient spring— Saint Govor's Well—on your left which is probably the origin of the 'swamp' Thoby and Vanessa thrilled Virginia as a child with. Once out of Kensington Gardens cross Kensington Road and turn left towards Knightsbridge. Only a few yards along you will find Hyde Park Gate. Ignore the first turning and you will arrive at a second Hyde Park Gate. Here at the bottom of this

narrow cul-de-sac which made Virginia feel rather claustro-
phobic, is number 22, a large white house, whose gable
tops its neighbours. You will also see that Baden-Powell
lived at number 9, Jacob Epstein at number 18 and
Winston Churchill at number 28.

You can catch a number of buses back to central
London from the park, or turn left out of Hyde Park
Gate and take a tube from Kensington High Street.

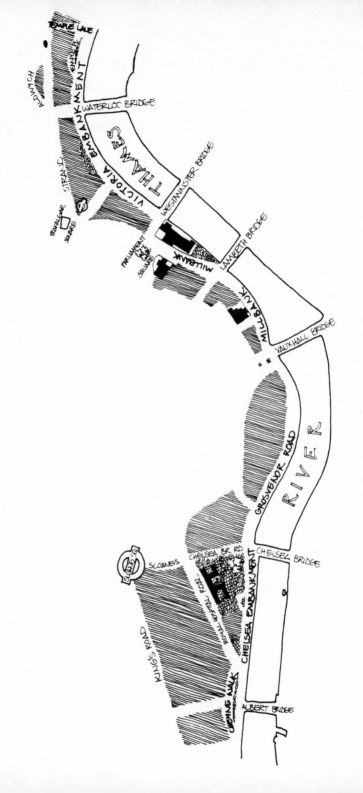

Walk 6

Ralph Denham's Walk
(from Temple to Cheyne Walk, along the
Embankment, in *Night and Day*)

Ralph Denham has just been to confide in Mary Datchet
that he is in love with her rival, Katharine Hilbery. Leav-
ing Mary's flat somewhere off the Fleet Street end of the
Strand, he walks a little way up Fleet Street to Temple
Lane on the right, which leads down to his friend
Rodney's flat in Temple Chambers. Failing to find
Rodney at home, and in a state of great agitation, Ralph
rushes off towards the river, probably down Middle
Temple Lane. The high strong wind, tossing clouds and
intermittent moonlight reflect his own excited mental
state and he decides to walk along the Embankment to
Katharine's house in Cheyne Walk. Exhausted by lack
of food and a day full of tramping about, he sits down
for a moment on the Victoria Embankment, before
setting off westwards for Chelsea.

   The best way to start this walk is by taking the tube
to Temple or Aldwych and making your way to Temple
Bar. Then follow Ralph down Middle Temple Lane,
through Temple Gardens to the Embankment. Turn
right along the river towards Westminster. Since you
will hopefully not be in such an agitated state as Ralph
was, you may like to note a number of interesting sites
on your way. Just before you reach Waterloo Bridge you
will see the massive outline of Somerset House on your
right, formerly one of the mansions which linked Westminster to the City before the two towns became united
as London. Between Waterloo and Hungerford Bridges
you will see Cleopatra's Needle, a relic from ancient
Egypt, and across the river you will see the outline of
the Royal Festival Hall. Between Hungerford and Westminster Bridges the skyline is dominated by the Houses
of Parliament, whose terraces will prevent you following

the river directly at this point. Instead you must do as
Ralph must have done and turn right into Bridge Street,
then left into Margaret Place, past the House of Commons, the House of Lords, along Abingdon Street to
Millbank. If you have not already done so, you might
digress to see Rodin's 'Burghers of Calais' in the Victoria
Tower Gardens. At the southern end of Lambeth Bridge
you will catch a glimpse of Lambeth Palace, the London
residence of the Archbishop of Canterbury. The least
attractive stretch of the Embankment, between Lambeth
and Vauxhall Bridges now follows, but you can enliven
it by popping in for a quick visit to the Tate Gallery of
Modern Art as you pass it on your right.

After Vauxhall Bridge the Embankment becomes
Grosvenor Road, where Leonard and Virginia used to
visit their Fabian friends, Sidney and Beatrice Webb.
Many of the old houses between Vauxhall and Chelsea
Bridges have been knocked down, but there are one or
two controversial modern developments to look out for,
notably Chelsea Reach on your left. Battersea Power
Station can also be seen across the river.

Chelsea Bridge and Battersea Power Station

By this stage of the journey Ralph was in a state of
extreme physical fatigue, which I hope you will not share:
the river, lights and houses became confused: 'details
merged themselves in the vaster prospect, of which the
flying gloom and the intermittent lights of lamp-posts
and private houses were the outward token'. Strengthened by his sense of walking in the direction of Katherine's

house, he carries on to Chelsea Bridge, along Chelsea
Embankment past Ranelagh Gardens. Walking more
slowly than he did, you should note the attractiveness
of both Chelsea and Albert Bridges, as well as Ranelagh
Gardens, where the Royal Horticultural Society's Annual
Flower Show is held. The gardens are part of the grounds
of the Royal Hospital, which was endowed by Charles II
and built by Christopher Wren from 1642 onwards,
specifically to house ex-servicemen, known today as
Chelsea Pensioners.

More history follows in the shape of the Chelsea
Physic Garden, one of the oldest botanic gardens in
Europe. Established in 1673 it remained a private garden
for centuries but has recently been opened to the public
and is well worth a visit. You have now only to cross
Royal Hospital Road and you have reached Ralph's
destination, Cheyne Walk.

For some yards before reaching the Hilbery's house

Ralph has been
'in a trance of
pleasure', but
once he reaches
it and pushes
open the gate
of the little
garden, he
hesitates: 'There
was no hurry,
however, for
the outside of
the house held
pleasure enough
to last him

Chelsea Physic Garden: detail of gate

some time longer. He crossed the road, and leant against
the balustrade of the Embankment, fixing his eyes upon
the house.' After gazing at the light flooding from the

three long windows of the drawing-room, which seems
to him beneficent yet 'so far above his level as to have
something austere about it', Ralph begins to tramp a
beat up and down the pavement before the Hilbery's
gate. Having walked so far he cannot bring himself to
knock and when the door opens to reveal William Rodney,
Ralph walks off with his rival back towards the City. Their
heated discussion of Katharine causes them to separate
after a short distance and one can only hope that Ralph
caught a bus home.

Cheyne Walk

Though we have no clear indication of which house
the Hilbery's lived in, beyond the three long first-floor
windows common to a number of them, Cheyne Walk
is full of interest in itself. Starting at number 4, you will
see that the novelist George Eliot died there in 1880.
Dante Gabriel Rossetti lived at number 16 from 1862
to 1882, when his house became a meeting place for artists and writers. The plaque on the side of number 23
informs us that King Henry VIII's manor house stood

on that spot until 1753, when it was demolished after the death of its last occupant, Sir Hans Sloane. Numbers 19 to 26 Cheyne Walk were built on its site between 1759 and 1765. The old manor house garden still lies beyond the end wall of Cheyne Mews and contains some mulberry trees said to have been planted by Queen Elizabeth I. Cheyne Walk continues beyond Oakley Street, but to my mind this section is not nearly so attractive. However, it does have its own literary interest, since both Henry James and T.S. Eliot lived at Carlyle Mansions at the end.

You may choose to return home via Oakley Street, where you can catch a bus to central London. Alternatively, you might wander back, by way of Cheyne Row, where Carlyle lived at number 24, and other side streets, most of which have their own blue plaques and charm. Your nearest tube is at Sloane Square at the end of King's Road.

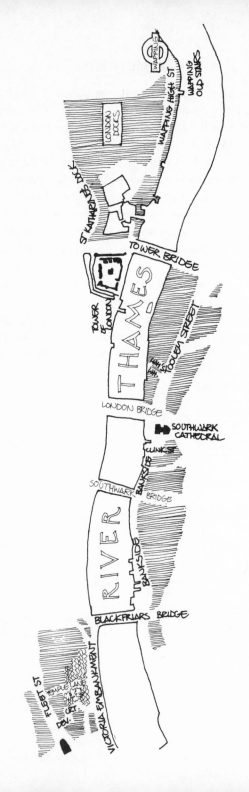

Walk 7

Mr and Mrs Ambrose's Walk
(from Waterloo to Wapping, in *The Voyage Out*)

The Voyage Out opens at Temple Bar, the meeting point
of Fleet Street and the Strand, with Mr and Mrs Ambrose
walking arm-in-arm down one of the narrow streets that
lead to the Embankment, much to the annoyance of the
busy lawyers' clerks and young lady typists trying to
pass them. Virginia, who knew the area well from her
time spent at the nearby Clifford's Inn, is probably thinking of Surrey Street, Essex Street or Arundel Street, since
the Ambroses emerge somewhere near Waterloo Bridge. I
prefer to start this walk by taking Devereux Court, down
through the Temple Gardens to the Embankment, a
narrower and more interesting way than the wider streets
to its west. Once at the Embankment Virginia places her
characters by having Mrs Ambrose fail to see the beauty
of Waterloo Bridge and 'the flats and churches and hotels
of Westminster' beyond, since her eyes are blinded with
tears at the thought of leaving her children. Roused
eventually by her husband from her misery, Mrs Ambrose
takes in the arches of Waterloo Bridge and the carts
moving across them, like a line of animals in a shooting
gallery. Her mood is further broken by the walk she now
takes towards Wapping, where they are to board their
ship for South America. As she walks towards Blackfriars
Bridge Mrs Ambrose reflects on London, which she has
inhabited, like Virginia, most of her life. The walk from
Blackfriars Bridge along Upper and Lower Thames Streets
has become an even more depressing experience than in
Mrs Ambrose's day. She felt the squalor so strongly at
this point in her journey that she decided to continue by
cab. Today the main problem is not so much squalor as
exhaust fumes and I suggest that you will enjoy this walk
a great deal more if you cross Blackfriars Bridge to the

Surrey side of the Thames, descend the steps to Hopton Street and follow the river eastwards along Bankside as far as Southwark Bridge. Not only will you avoid the cars, you will also have a magnificent view of most of the City churches, including St Bride's, St Martin Ludgate, St Paul's, St Augustine's, St Nicholas Cole Abbey, St Mary Somerset, St Mary-le-Bow and St Mary Alderney.

Just before you reach Southwark Bridge you will also see on your right at Cardinal Wharf the house in which Sir Christopher Wren is believed to have lived whilst he was building St Paul's Cathedral, which lies directly opposite. He was rowed to work daily, one assumes. Luckily, this charming house, which also served as a refuge for Catherine of Aragon when she landed in England in 1502 to marry Henry VIII, has been preserved. Most of the buildings in this area have been demolished to make way for new developments, such as the International Shakespeare Centre now under construction. Another historic survivor, just east of Southwark Bridge, is the Anchor, where you may like to stop for a drink on the river terrace.

Christopher Wren's house

The Anchor marks the end of Bankside, but Clink Street continues to run very near the river and it also takes you past the ruins of an ancient church on your right and to St Saviour's Dock, with its old sailing ship, the *Kathleen and May*. Follow Cathedral Street round to your right and you will come to Southwark Cathedral, which is well worth a visit. Turn back towards the river along Montague Close, which will lead to Tooley Street. Here, apart from a diversion at Hay's Wharf to see the

dramatic new shopping complex and *HMS Belfast*, you
have reached the worst part of your journey. You may,
like Mrs Ambrose, decide to take public transport along
this stretch as far as Tower Bridge Road. If you are beginning to flag you may like to take the 78 bus as far as
the Tower itself, though it would be a pity to miss the
walk across the bridge. There will almost certainly be a
walkway the whole length of the river between Blackfriars and Tower Bridges quite soon, so check to see if
it has opened by the time you read this.

You are now on the last lap of this walk to Wapping
and if you are already tired, you can stop at the Tower.
However, the walk through the newly renovated St
Katharine's Dock and along Wapping High Street is
worth the extra effort. You simply cross Tower Bridge
at the Tower end, descend the steps to St Katharine's

Wapping Pier Head

215

Way and thread your way through the yacht haven to
Wapping High Street. Do not be put off by the derelict
start to the High Street but persist until you reach the
elegant square of eighteenth-century houses at Wapping
Pierhead and, shortly afterwards, Wapping Old Stairs,
which still lead straight into the river. It was to Wapping
Old Stairs that Orlando went as a lusty youth to flirt
with innkeepers' daughters and chat with sailors. It was
almost certainly the place where Mr and Mrs Ambrose
found a small boat to take them to their ship, judging
from Virginia's reference to 'the monstrous outline' of

Tower Bridge and her vivid description of the scene:

> At this point the cab stopped, for it was in danger of
> being crushed like an egg-shell. The wide Embankment
> which had had room for cannon-balls and squadrons,
> had now shrunk to a cobbled lane steaming with smells
> of malt and oil and blocked by waggons. While her
> husband read the placards pasted on the brick
> announcing the hours at which certain ships would
> sail for Scotland, Mrs Ambrose did her best to find
> information. From a world exclusively occupied in
> feeding waggons with sacks, half obliterated too in a
> fine yellow fog, they got neither help nor attention.
> It seemed a miracle when an old man approached,
> guessed their condition, and proposed to row them
> out to their ship in the little boat which he kept moor-
> ed at the bottom of a flight of steps.

The pub next to Wapping Old Stairs, the Town of Rams-
gate, almost certainly provided refreshment in the
Ambroses' day for passengers arriving or departing from
them. It still does so and makes a very attractive place to
stop for lunch or a drink. There is also a tube station
further along the High Street to take you back to central
London. Alternatively, you can retrace your steps to
Tower Hill and catch a bus or tube there.

Suggested Side Trips

Apart from these suggested London walks round Virginia Woolf country, there are a number of other interesting trips for the enthusiastic. A visit to Richmond makes a pleasant Sunday outing. You can start by seeing Virginia's first Richmond home at 17 The Green, where she and Leonard had rooms on the first floor. There was no tradesman's entrance to Boots spoiling the ground floor in their day; otherwise the house remains unchanged. If you now cross the town's main square you will find Paradise Road, a name Virginia would have appreciated. A few hundred yards up on the left is Hogarth House, the righthand side of which the Woolfs inhabited from 1915 to 1924. You might finish your trip off by taking a walk Virginia often did — 'through the Park, down the avenue and back by the river'. She was probably referring to the Old Deer Park. Another favourite walk was to Kew Gardens, a name she gave to one of her earliest short stories written while she was living in Richmond and hand-printed by her and Leonard in 1919.

If you are feeling more adventurous you might like to visit Virginia's houses in Sussex, namely Little Talland, Asham, The Round House, Monk's House, and her sister's house, Charleston. Directions are given in Part 5. The Friends of Charleston have organised several walks from Monk's House to Charleston, though there is unfortunately no room to give full details here. However, it is worthwhile keeping an eye on the *Charleston Newsletter* for future walks of that kind.

Finally, for the very energetic or totally dedicated, a trip to see Talland House, at St Ives in Cornwall, is mandatory.

5
Virginia Woolf's Other Houses

Talland House, St Ives, Cornwall
(1882-1894)

When Virginia's father discovered St Ives on a walking
tour in 1881, he liked it so much he rented a house own-
ed by the Great Western Railway, which had just opened
a branch line to the small Cornish town. Talland House,
as it was called, became the Stephens' holiday home from
1882, the first year of Virginia's life, to 1895, the year of
her mother's tragic death. The house stood high above
Carbis Bay, with a magnificent view of the sea. It was
sufficiently near the railway station, both for transport-
ing Leslie and Julia's enormous household and for meeting
the many friends who descended on them every summer.
The signal announcing the arrival of a train could be seen
from the garden of Talland House and as soon as the
Stephens saw it go down, they would rush off to meet
whichever friend or relative was due.

Virginia remembered Talland as square, like a child's
drawing of a house, remarkable only for its flat roof
and the railings with crossed bars of wood that ran round
it. Though a little more ornamental than this suggests,
the main attraction of Talland House was not its
architecture but its view right across the bay to Godrevy
lighthouse.

The thirteen summers Virginia spent at St Ives were
among the happiest, if not the happiest, of her life. She
loved the wild Cornish landscape — Clody and Halestown
Bog, Carbis Bay, Lelant, Zennor, Trevail, The Gurnard's
Head were all names she conjured with afterwards. She
adored the visits to the beach, which she describes vividly

at the beginning of *Jacob's Room*, the sound of the sea and the sight of the lighthouse flashing, which make *To the Lighthouse* so memorable, and visits to the steep little town, which Mr Tansley records in living detail in the same book. When Virginia's parents took Talland House she believed they gave her something invaluable, which none of her subsequent visits to Surrey, Sussex or the Isle of Wight could ever live up to.

Besides the landscape and the house, with its prominent bay windows, attic rooms and balconies, another aspect Virginia recorded in faithful detail, particularly in her largely autobiographical *To the Lighthouse*, was the garden. Set on a steep slope it had many different areas for the children to explore. There were the little lawns surrounded by fragrant escallonias, the 'coffee' garden, the fountain, the strawberry bed, the kitchen garden, the pond, the big tree, the cricket ground and the 'love corner' beneath the greenhouse, where Leo Maxse had proposed to another guest, Kitty Lushington, among the Jackmanii.

Altogether, Talland House left Virginia with an incurably romantic feeling for Cornwall: 'I see children running in the garden. A Spring day. Life so new. People so enchanting. The sound of the sea at night'. Her strong sense of what she called the poetry of existence was often connected with the sea and St Ives. So that it is no surprise to find their influence in her work. The most obvious debt is in *To the Lighthouse* which, in spite of her transparent device of placing the Ramsays' holiday home in Scotland, is a largely autobiographical reconstruction of Talland House. The lighthouse itself is based on Godrevy lighthouse which Virginia could see from her bedroom window every childhood holiday. There is a reference in *The Hyde Park Gate News* of 12 September 1892 to Thoby and Virginia having been invited to visit the lighthouse and to Adrian's bitter disappointment at

10. *Talland House, St Ives, Cornwall*: Virginia's family holiday home for the first thirteen years of her life.

not being allowed to go too. Mr Carmichael in *To the Lighthouse* is probably based on a regular visitor to Talland House, Mr Wolstenhome, a brilliant mathematician but worldly failure who took opium. Even the return visit of the motherless Ramsay family after ten years is based on the Stephen children's own return to Talland House ten years after their mother's death.

Jacob's Room also contains a long opening section based on St Ives' beach and a later section reflecting Virginia's detailed knowledge and love of Cornwall, when Jacob visits the Durrants' holiday home there.

Finally, and most pervasively, *The Waves* is a direct tribute to Virginia's dependence on the sea, which had penetrated her awareness so early and so deeply at Talland House:

> If life has a base that it stands upon, if it is a bowl that one fills and fills and fills—then my bowl without a doubt stands upon this memory. It is of lying half asleep, half awake, in bed in the nursery at St Ives. It is of hearing the waves breaking, one, two, one, two, and sending a splash of water over the beach; and then breaking, one, two, one, two, behind a yellow blind. It is of hearing the blind draw its little acorn across the floor as the wind blew the blind out. It is of lying and hearing this splash and seeing this light, and feeling, it is almost impossible that I should be here; of feeling the purest ecstasy I can conceive.

Talland House still stands, very little altered, and you may reach it by train or car to St Ives, where it is only a few hundred yards from the station.

Little Talland House, Firle, Sussex
(1911-1912)

Though Leslie Stephen continued to rent summer houses for his large family after Julia's death in 1895, he never again did so on a long lease. It was not until Virginia grew up and rented her own country house that we find her once more visiting one particular place regularly. Though her new retreat was not in Cornwall, she christened it Little Talland House in the hope perhaps of recreating the happy atmosphere of her childhood holiday home.

Little Talland House was at Firle in Sussex, which Virginia had got to know gradually over the years. She had visited friends, the Freshfields, at Forest Row, in the middle of 1908 and again in May 1909, by which time she had grown to love the South Downs. At any rate, when her doctor advised her, after another breakdown in 1910, to look for a place to relax, she chose Sussex. She and Adrian spent the Christmas of that year at Lewes, looking for a house for her to rent and, by the end of 1910, she had found one at Firle. Early in 1911 she took possession.

Little Talland House, though set in the middle of the beautiful Sussex Downs, was the least attractive of Virginia's country houses and it is not surprising that she left it without regret after only one year. It had been built only six years earlier when she saw it in 1910 and must have looked painfully new among the other mellower, more attractive houses in Firle's small high street. Red brick on the ground floor and stuccoed with mock Tudor beams running through the first and attic floors, Little Talland had not even the advantage of being detached. Two gables dominated two 'semis', each with their own patch of front, side and back garden. By September 1911 Virginia, who had had time to explore the picturesque villages around Firle, described Little

11. *Little Talland House, Firle, Sussex*: the first country house Virginia rented.

Talland as 'not a cottage, but a hideous suburban villa'.
It was a convenient base for her long walks on the downs,
but no more. So that when she and Leonard Woolf discovered a beautiful old house not far from Firle, she
left Little Talland as quickly as possible.

In spite of its lack of architectural merit, Little Talland
is worth a visit. Lewes is the nearest large town, where
you take the A27 road towards Eastbourne. Firle is a
turning off on your right, just past a sign on your left to
Glynde, Ringmer and Glyndbourne. Little Talland is
quite near the beginning of the village street, opposite
the village Reading Room.

Asham House, near Itford, Sussex (1912-1919)

Virginia and Leonard discovered Asham House* in October 1911 on a walk over the downs from Firle to the
Ouse Valley. By then Leonard was already half in love
with Virginia, which is possibly why he saw Asham—their
mutual discovery—as an 'extraordinarily romantic-looking
house'. The pursuit and renting of Asham certainly
brought them together. By the time Virginia held her
house-warming party there from 3rd-5th February 1912,
Leonard had become a regular weekend visitor. It was at
Asham that they came to know each other more closely
and to discover their shared love of walking and reading.
By May 1912 Virginia had agreed to marry Leonard, and
did so in August. Though Virginia had originally asked
Vanessa to share the lease of Asham with her, she and
Leonard seem to have taken it over completely very
early on.

Asham was set in a hollow of the downs, separated
from the main Lewes-Seaford road by a large field of
sheep. It faced due west and from its front windows
*Sometimes spelt Asheham, or Ascham.

and terraces you looked across the field and the Ouse valley to the line of downs on the west of the river. Behind the house was a steep hill and to the south and north were rows of elms running down each side of the field to the road.

Asham had been built originally as a 'gentleman's residence'. When the neighbouring Itford Farm had been bought by a Lewes solicitor in about 1820, he built Asham as a summer retreat. One of the present occupiers says that the house itself was finished in about 1825. By contrast with Little Talland, Asham is an extremely elegant, though not perhaps very practical, house, especially for only two people. It is L-shaped and, in 1912, had two large sitting-rooms on the ground floor, four bedrooms on the first and a vast attic above. Its flat front, relieved only by the curves of its striking double-arched stone windows was, according to Leonard, yellow-washed. Large french windows opened on to a small terrace, which in turn led straight on to a lawn sloping down to the field. At each side of the main building were single-storey wings, one of them intended as a music room.

Asham has not changed externally since 1912, except that it is now painted white rather than washed yellow. Inside it has been divided into two dwellings and the large attic subdivided to provide more rooms. Even the cement workings, which finally began to ruin Asham in Virginia's eyes, have crept back from the house, leaving it very much as it must have been in 1912. The legends of Asham being haunted, which were the germ of Virginia's short story 'A Haunted House', have also sur-vived and are firmly believed by its present occupants.

Virginia and Leonard loved Asham, both for its physical beauties and the sense of tranquility it gave them. When Virginia describes coming in from a walk and sit-ting down for a read by the fire, she is focussing perhaps

12. *Asham House, Near Itford,
Sussex*: the house Virginia and
Leonard discovered whilst walk-
ing on the South Downs.

on the reason Asham suited them both so much: it catered to their two predominant needs, reading and walking. Leonard wrote, nearly fifty years after leaving Asham: 'I have never known a house which had such a strong character, personality of its own — romantic, gentle, melancholy, lovely'. When Virginia suffered another of her breakdowns in 1913, it was to Asham she went to recover.

So that when the landlord decided not to renew their lease of Asham in 1919, but to live in it himself with his elderly mother, both Virginia and Leonard were very depressed. In spite of one serious inconvenience — its lack of sun — they could not imagine a more peaceful place. It was therefore most unwillingly that they started searching for another country house in the summer of 1919.

Asham House is a few miles west of Little Talland. From Firle you must return to the A27, as if going back into Lewes, then take the first main turning on your left, the A26 to Newhaven and Seaford. Just beyond Beddingham and before you reach Itford, you will see cement workings on your left. Running along the side of these is an avenue of trees, which leads to Asham.

The Round House, Lewes, Sussex
(June-July 1919)

The Round House, Lewes, is the least known of all Virginia's country houses, understandably so, since she never lived there. It was bought on an impulse when Virginia was searching desperately for an alternative to Asham and sold just as impulsively when she realised that for whatever reason Leonard didn't take to it. So quickly did this take place, that contracts were probably never exchanged.

Yet the Round House had, and still has, great charm.
Perched on the western walls of the Castle near the centre
of Lewes, it is, as its name suggests, completely round,
though a small two-storey addition has been added since
Virginia first saw it. As its plaque informs us, the Round
House was erected as a windmill in 1802, but the mill
was removed to Racehill in about 1835 and the truncat-
ed building converted to a cottage. Virginia's description
of how she discovered it vividly conveys its appeal, as
well as telling one how she found it:

> Off I went up Pipes Passage, under the clock, and saw
> rising at the top of the sloping path a singular shaped
> roof, rising into a point, and spreading out in a circular
> petticoat all round it. . . . An elderly and humble
> cottage woman the owner, showed me over. How far
> my satisfaction with the small rooms, and the view,
> and the ancient walls, and the wide sitting room, and
> the general oddity and character of the whole place
> were the result of finding something that would do,
> that one could conceive living in, that was cheap (free-
> hold £300) I don't know; but as I inspected the rooms
> I became conscious of a rising desire to settle here . . .
> I liked the way the town dropped from the garden
> leaving us on a triangular island, vegetables one side,
> grass the other; the path encircling the round house
> amused me; . . . Lewes that afternoon, with its many
> trees and laburnums, and water meadows, and sunny
> bow windowed houses, and broad High Street looked
> very tempting and dignified.

To be fair to Leonard, both he and Virginia wanted a
house in the country not the town, and one with more
rooms and a bigger garden than the Round House posses-
sed. Yet it is not difficult, even after nearly seventy
years to see why it appealed to Virginia, whose appreciat-

13. *The Round House, Pipes Passage, Lewes, Sussex*: the house Virginia bought but never lived in.

ion of oddity was strong. It is worth a visit to this little cottage which, except for its small addition, remains very much as Virginia saw it in June 1919. Pipes Passage lies about half-way along Lewes High Street on the same side as the castle.

Monk's House, Rodmell, Sussex (1919-1941)

As Virginia took Leonard to inspect the Round House in Lewes at the end of June 1919, they noticed a placard on the wall of an auctioneer's office: 'Lot 1. Monks House, Rodmell. An old fashioned house standing in three-quarters of an acre of land to be sold with possession'. Leonard murmured, 'That would have suited us exactly'. So that when it became clear that he did not want to take the Round House, Virginia decided to visit Monk's House the following day. Having been too enthusiastic about the Round House, she was determined this time to see all the disadvantages. The rooms were small; the kitchen unsatisfactory; there was an oil stove and no grate; there was no hot water, no bath and no lavatory, only an earth-closet. Yet in spite of her determination to remain cool, she could not help being excited by the old chimney piece; the niches for holy water and, above all, the garden. Its size, shape, fertility and wildness made her forget all criticism. She immediately wanted to own Monk's House. Leonard's response when he visited Rodmell the next day, though more balanced than Virginia's was no less enthusiastic. The garden alone, with its ample orchard, and patchwork quilt of trees, shrubs, flowers, vegetables, fruit, roses, crocus, cabbages and currant bushes delighted the gardener in him. He and Virginia decided on the spot to buy Monk's House if they could and, after much nail-biting, bought it at auction for £700, a full £100 under their limit.

After a last August at Asham, they took possession of Monk's House on 1 September 1919 and spent the month there. In subsequent years they spent at least two months every summer as well as Christmas, Easter and most alternate weekends. They finally went to live at Rodmell shortly after war broke out in 1939 and were still living there when Virginia walked out to drown herself in the nearby Ouse in March 1941. Her ashes were buried at the foot of a great elm tree on the bank of the lawn in the garden. In spite of such traumatic associations, Leonard kept Monk's House until his own death there in 1969.

Monk's House had none of what Virginia called 'the flawless beauty' of Asham. An 'unpretending' house, it was long and low with one side fronting Rodmell's main street and weatherboarded on that side. In 1919 the street in front of the house was little more than a cart track running out to the flats of the water-meadows. Nevertheless, Monk's House was, and is, an appealing house particularly inside, where its oak-beamed rooms indicate its age. It was said to date from the fifteenth or sixteenth century and to have got its name from belonging to the monks of Lewes Priory, who used it for their retreats. Both Virginia and Leonard had their doubts about this, though they liked to believe it. When they first saw Monk's House most of what had been fairly large rooms were partitioned into eight or nine smaller ones. They removed these partitions immediately and, in the course of time, added a kitchen, bathroom, sitting-room, another bedroom and, most importantly of all, built a simple wooden hut in the garden for Virginia. It was here she wrote out many of her most famous novels, starting with *Jacob's Room*, for she found Monk's House particularly conducive to writing.

When Virginia was not writing in the country, she was either reading or walking and Monk's House offered even

14. *Monk's House, Rodmell,*
Sussex: Virginia and Leonard's
country house for twenty-two
years. Virginia committed
suicide in the nearby Ouse in
1941.

better walks than Asham. It lies off a minor road leading
from Lewes to Newhaven, which at Rodmell runs nearly
parallel across the Ouse with the major A26 from Lewes
to Newhaven.

Travelling by car from London you take the A22 to
East Grinstead, then the A275 to Lewes. On the outskirts
of Lewes follow the signs for the A27 to Brighton. Just
before you reach the A27, you will see a signpost point-
ing off on your left to Kingston, Iford and Rodmell. The
village and Monk's House are in a turning on your left
just after the pub. Monk's House is the last house on
the right and has a National Trust sign outside. It is
open to the public on Wednesdays and Saturdays from
2-6 p.m. from April to October inclusive. There is an
entrance fee.

Charleston, Firle, Sussex (1916-1941)

There is one other house which, though not strictly
speaking Virginia's, was so much a part of her life in the
country that it could certainly be called her territory. It
is also well worth a visit for its own interest. Charleston,
the house rented by Virginia's sister Vanessa from September 1916 onwards, is a mellow farmhouse, mainly
eighteenth century though parts of it date back to the
previous century. It is brick built and rendered. It was
Virginia who first urged Vanessa to take Charleston,
which was about a mile from Firle. When it became clear
that Vanessa and Duncan Grant would have to leave
Wisset in Suffolk where they had been trying fruit-farm-
ing as an alternative to conscription, Virginia was determined to find them a house near Asham. Leonard was
duly sent to inspect Charleston and pronounced it 'a
most delightful house', though he seems to have had
more to say about the garden, as Virginia reports it to

Vanessa: 'It has a charming garden, with a pond, and fruit trees, and vegetables, all now rather run wild, but you could make it lovely. The house is very nice, with large rooms, and one room with big windows fit for a studio'. In fact once Vanessa and Duncan moved in the whole house became their studio. Apart from their official studios, they painted almost everything in sight— walls, bedsteads, cupboards, tables, doors, chairs, plates, fireplaces, shutters and any other surface they could find.

Charleston was large and rambling enough to suit the many other needs of Vanessa's strange *ménage*. There were not only studios for herself and Duncan to find, but a library for her husband Clive Bell, a sitting-room and dining room as well as bedrooms for themselves, their three children and the numerous guests who stayed for varying lengths of time. Accommodation was also needed for the servants who came and went rather stormily during the first decade. (After that Grace Higgins came and stayed for the next fifty years.)

From the outside the house has a calmer, more regular, air than Vanessa's life-style suggests. It is far more classical than Monk's House, but less elegant than Asham. Six windows and a door dominate the front, with dormer windows indicating a fair number of attic rooms in the steep red-tiled roof. It looks a comfortable, lived-in house and one can see why it suited Vanessa and Duncan ideally. Both remained there till their respective deaths in 1961 and 1978.

After Duncan's death, when his daughter Angelica was about to leave Charleston, it was spotted by a London art dealer, Deborah Gage, who immediately set about preserving it for posterity. She founded the Charleston Trust, a charitable foundation dedicated to restoring and maintaining the house and garden.

To reach Charleston, you should take the A27 out of

15. *Charleston, Firle, Sussex*:
the house Leonard discovered
for Virginia's sister, Vanessa
Bell, who lived and painted
there with Duncan Grant from
1916 to their respective deaths
in 1961 and 1978.

Lewes in the Eastbourne direction. After passing the turning on your right to Firle Place and the Middle Farm Shop on your left, you must take the next right turn. The first lane on your right leads up to Charleston. The lane immediately opposite on your left leads to Tilton. This was the house bought by Maynard Keynes and his wife, the Russian ballerina Lydia Lopokova, to be near their Bloomsbury friends in the country. Charleston is now open to the public on Wednesdays, Thursdays, Saturdays and Sundays, 2-6 p.m., April to October inclusive. There is an entrance fee.

Bibliography

Bell, Quentin. *Virginia Woolf: A Biography* (2 volumes), The Hogarth Press, 1972.

Brewster, Dorothy. *Virginia Woolf's London*, George Allen and Unwin, 1959.

The Charleston Newsletter, edited by Hugh Lee.

Daiches, David. 'Virginia Woolf's London' in *Literary Landscapes of the British Isles*, Paddington Press, 1979.

Edel, Leon. *Bloomsbury: A House of Lions*, Penguin Books, 1981.

Lehmann, John. *Virginia Woolf and Her World*, Thames and Hudson, 1975.

Rosenbaum, S.P. (ed.) *The Bloomsbury Group: A Collection of Memoirs, Commentary and Criticism*, University of Toronto Press, 1975.

Spalding, Frances. *Vanessa Bell*, Weidenfeld and Nicholson, 1984.

Woolf, Leonard. *Beginning Again: An Autobiography of the Years 1911 to 1918*, The Hogarth Press, 1964.

.. .. *Sowing: An Autobiography of the Years 1880 to 1904*, The Hogarth Press, 1960.

Woolf, Virginia. *The Diaries of Virginia Woolf*, volumes I-V, The Hogarth Press, 1977-1984.

.. .. *Jacob's Room*, The Hogarth Press, 1922.

.. .. *The Letters of Virginia Woolf*, volumes I-VI, Chatto and Windus, 1975-1980.

.. .. *The London Scene*, The Hogarth Press, 1982.

.. .. *Moments of Being*, Triad Granada, 1978.

.. .. *Mrs Dalloway*, The Hogarth Press, 1925.

.. .. *Night and Day*, Duckworth, 1919.

.. .. *Orlando: A Biography*, The Hogarth

Press, 1928.

.. ..   *To the Lighthouse*, The Hogarth Press,
          1927.

.. ..   *The Voyage Out*, Duckworth, 1915.

.. ..   *The Waves*, The Hogarth Press, 1931.

.. ..   *The Years*, The Hogarth Press, 1937.

Index